D1882679

THE STORY

OF

THE GREAT WAR

Owing to the antiquity and rarity of this book, certain pages are regrettably absent, and readability is compromised due to the blurring of the original text. If you possess any insights regarding the availability of these missing sections, kindly inform us. Your assistance is crucial in ensuring the completion of this significant work for the benefit of future generations.

THE STORY

OF

THE GREAT WAR

SOME LESSONS FROM THE MAHABHARATA

FOR THE USE OF HINDU STUDENTS IN
THE SCHOOLS OF INDIA

ANNIE BESANT

GYAN

Published by

GYAN

Gyan Publishing House
5, Ansari Road
Daryaganj, New Delhi-110002
Phone: 011-47034999, 9811692060
E-mail: books@gyanbooks.com

Distribution Network
gyanbooks.com
India, USA, Canada, UK, Australia

© Publisher

All rights reserved. No part of this work may be reproduced, stored, adapted, or transmitted in any form or by any means, electronic, mechanical, photocopying, micro-filming, recording or otherwise, or translated in any language, without the prior written permission of the copyright owner and the publisher.

ISBN: 978-93-6780-183-3 (PB)
First Published, 1899

2nd Impression 2024

Printed at: Gyan Press, Delhi.

The book is sold subject to the condition that it shall not, by way of trade or otherwise, be lent, resold, hired out, or otherwise circulated without the prior publisher's written consent.

THE STORY OF THE GREAT WAR
Author: ANNIE BESANT

THE STORY

OF

THE GREAT WAR

SOME LESSONS FROM THE MAHÂBHÂRATA

FOR THE USE OF HINDU STUDENTS IN THE SCHOOLS OF INDIA

BY

ANNIE BESANT, F. T. S.

FROM NOTES OF LECTURES ORIGINALLY DELIVERED AT THE CENTRAL HINDU COLLEGE, BENARES.

THEOSOPHICAL PUBLISHING SOCIETY, BENARES.
THEOSOPHIST OFFICE, ADYAR, MADRAS.
THEOSOPHICAL PUBLISHING SOCIETY, 26 CHARING CROSS. LONDON.

1899.

CONTENTS.

THE STORY
OF
THE GREAT WAR

CHAPTER I.

INTRODUCTION

WE are going to study the book called the "Mahâbhârata", one of the greatest books in the world. To do this usefully, we must begin by seeing what sort of book it is that we are going to study, and what sort of mind we are to bring to the reading of it. For the mind of the student has a great deal to do with understanding the book. If his mind be properly prepared he will understand more easily the book he is going to read, than if he comes to it with his mind in a wrong attitude. If you want to see a thing, you must look at it with your eyes open, not shut. You must turn your face to it, not your back. And so with the mind; its eyes must be opened and its face turned to the book. We must know how to read it, and what principles are taken for granted in it. So we will begin by getting our minds ready, and putting them into the right attitude.

We must find out how to read our book. Then we shall take up Parva after Parva (volume after volume), picking out the most important parts and stringing them into an orderly story. We shall try to get a clear idea of the whole book—what it is meant to teach, the kind of people whose story is told in it, what they were doing and trying to do, how the Gods helped or hindered them, and the working of the Gods in the events that took place.

When you go out into the world you will meet people who do not believe that Gods are shaping events, and guiding the worlds. Those who do not believe in the Hindu religion will also attack your Scriptures, your sacred books. It is therefore part of the duty of a Hindu boy to understand a little about the sacred books of his religion, so that he may not be shaken by what ignorant or foolish people may say against them.

The "Mahâbhârata" has a high value as literature, that is, when judged from a literary standpoint. Every nation has a literature—books—and some stand high and some low in this respect. They have poems, histories, stories, philosophic and religious books. The place that a nation holds in the mind of the world depends very largely on its books. If a nation produces great books, that nation is looked on as great by other nations. If it has no great books, it is despised. There is no nation which has greater books than the Indian.

You read about the Greeks, with their poet Homer who told the story of a ten-years' war, and with many splendid writers of philosophy and history. People now read their books and say, what a great country Greece was to produce such writers. People in the West are beginning to read your books written in Sanskrit, and to say what a great nation the Indians must have been in the old days to write such books. The "Mahâbhârata" is the greatest poem in the whole world. There is no other poem so splendid as this, so full of what we want to know, and of what it is good for us to study. It is so beautiful in its language and tells so interesting a story, that every Hindu boy should know something about it. It is not good to grow up without knowing a little of this greatest poem in the world, written by and for your own fore-fathers. So we are going to begin its study.

There are three things in which its greatness chiefly consists: (*a*) Its Ethics; (*b*) Its Philosophy; (*c*) Its History.

(*a*) Ethics means morality dealt with systematically—good conduct, and the rules of good conduct

When you learn arithmetic you are given certain rules, and if you follow the rules and apply them properly, the sum comes out right. So it is with ethics, the science of morality. It deals with right and wrong, what it is good to do and what it is bad to do. There are definite rules. Ethics does not say: "You ought to be good," or "You ought not to be bad;" but it gives rules, showing what is good and what is bad, what you should do and what you should avoid. All these rules and the principles underlying them are called Ethics.

The "Mahâbhârata" is great as a teacher of Ethics, showing us how to behave ourselves. It teaches everybody. It teaches children, boys and girls, men and women, and it teaches them what to do at each part of life. It teaches Brâhmaṇas, Kshattriyas, Vaishyas, Shûdras, and people without caste as well, so that all may learn how to behave themselves in everyday life. It teaches how to live in business, in the family, as husband, father and son, wife, mother and daughter. It teaches the common things of everyday life, and does this in a very interesting way by means of stories. Instead of saying: "You ought to tell the truth", it tells us a number of stories about people who told the truth and what happened to them. Instead of saying: "You ought not to tell a lie," it tells us a number of stories about people who told lies and what happened to them. In this way we learn how to apply the rules of conduct, and thus to understand them much better. When one of your professors teaches you a rule in arithmetic, he gives you a number of sums to be worked out by that rule, and that helps you to understand it much better than if you had only the rule and no examples.

Good behaviour is a more important thing than some people think; success, happiness and prosperity depend on it. There is a story about Prahlâda, who, by the merit of his good conduct, took from Indra the sovereignty of the three worlds; then Indra, disguising himself as a Brâhmaṇa, went and served Prahlâda as his disciple, until Prahlâda, pleased with him, offered to grant any boon he desired. Then Indra asked that Prahlâda would give him his behaviour; and, though filled with fear as to the consequences, Prahlâda gave it, bound by his word. As Prahlâda sat, brooding over what had occurred, a flame with a shadowy form issued from his body, and when the king asked, "Who art thou?" the form answered: "I am the embodiment of thy Behaviour, cast off by thee. I am going away to dwell with thy devoted disciple the Brâhmaṇa." And another form left the king's body, and, when asked, said: "I am Righteousness; I live where Behaviour dwells." And in the same way went forth Truth, Good Deeds, Might and Prosperity; and the last named said: "O Prahlâda, it was by thy Behaviour that thou hadst reduced the three worlds to subjection. Knowing this, the chief of the celestials robbed thee of thy Behaviour. Righteousness, Truth, Good Deeds, Might and myself, O thou of great wisdom, all have our root verily in Behaviour." And then Prosperity went whither Behaviour had gone. (*Shânti Parva*, § 124.)

Another important principle we learn from many stories in the "Mahâbhârata" is that morality is relative. This means, that what is right conduct for one person is not always right conduct for another, and that duty depends on what a man is. If you are a boy, it is right for you to do what your teacher tells you. If you are a teacher, it is right for you to tell others what to do. If you are a father, it is your duty to train your sons. If you are a son, it is your duty to follow your father's advice. The usefulness of a man depends on his knowing and doing the duties belonging to his place in life. To you, as boys in school and college, it is not of importance to know the duties of the head of a household. It is very important that you should know and do your duties as students,

The "Mahâbhârata" lays great stress on this relation between conduct and position.

Further, this book gives all that is needed by everybody in the way of moral teaching. Some books are meant only for special people. A very difficult book is only for a learned man; the ignorant man cannot understand it. A law book is useful to a pleader, useless to a peasant. Some books on religion are only for advanced people. But this book is for everybody, and however little a man may know, there is something for him here. It can be read by everybody, and everybody can profit by it. If they read no other book, they can learn from this all they need in religious and moral knowledge.

(*b*) Philosophy is addressed to the Intellect, the reasoning and judging power in man. It deals with truths about God, man, the world, and the universe, and arranges these things in an intellectual system. The "Mahâbhârata" teaches a great philosophy, that which underlies all the Hindu religion. There is one Supreme Being, God, the one Self in everybody and in everything. This God is everywhere, in the sun, moon and stars, in Gods and men, in animals, vegetables and minerals. There is one life in all, and that life is God. Therefore all creatures are one; they are not really separate; what is good for one is good for all; what is good for all is good for one. Because of this, we should be kind to all and love all; there is a common life, and we hurt it in ourselves when we hurt it in another. The life in the ox, in the bird, is your life, is yours. You should take care of it and protect it as your own. Let me tell you the story about king Ushinâra and the pigeon who sought his protection. The chief duty of a king is to protect all in his kingdom, and two of the Gods, Indra and Agni, wished to test Ushinâra in his discharge of this duty. Indra took the form of a hawk, Agni of a pigeon, and the pigeon, chased by the hawk, took refuge in the king's lap. The hawk demanded the pigeon as his lawful prey, but the king refused, on the ground that the hawk had sought his protection. Then the hawk argued that, deprived of food, he would perish, and that in protecting one life the king failed to protect many. The king, refusing to give up the pigeon, offered other food, but all was refused, until at last the hawk offered to give up his claim if the king would give of his own flesh as much as equalled the weight of the pigeon. The king gladly consented, and placed a piece of his own flesh in the balance against the weight of the pigeon; but the scale rose. So he cut off piece after piece, and still the pigeon was the heavier, until at last he placed his own mangled figure in the scale. Then the Gods revealed themselves, and blessed the king who saved a suppliant at the cost of his own flesh. (*Vana Parva*, § 130, 131.)

(*c*) The "Mahâbhârata" is a history, although it is more than a history. This big book in eighteen volumes tells a story about things that really occurred some five thousand years ago. Five thousand years ago Shrî Krishṇa, the Blessed Lord, put off His mortal body. Then began the Kali Yuga. The story told in this book ends soon after He left the earth. That is the first thing to understand. This is not a fairy-tale, but a history. The mighty Kshattriya caste, the warrior-caste of India, was for the most part destroyed in the Great War. Her soldiers that kept her safe, and made an iron wall around her, were slain in this war, and that caste ceased to exist as a powerful order, and was carried on only by scattered families. Its destruction opened the way for India's conquest and fall.

The Kali Yuga is a time in which people lose belief in the Gods and their work, and become more and more the servants of outer things. They believe in the things that they can see, hear, touch, taste or smell—the things your bodily senses tell you about. You believe in a table, because you can see and touch it. You believe in a house, a person, the objects round you, because you can see and handle them. But many people do not believe in things that they cannot see or touch, in Gods that are round us all the time, in the Supreme Self whose Life is our life. Most people here are half-way. They will not say they do not believe in the Gods, but their lives show that they do not believe in them. The things that are done by the Gods every day among us are not seen as their work. You talk of nature, of the sun rising, the moon shining, the water running, the fire burning. These things are matters of course. But in every one of them a God is at work. When the fire burns—on the hearth, in the jungle—a God is at work, and the fire is his way of showing himself. The fire is not a mere chemical thing, but it is the way the God Agni has of showing himself down here. In other worlds he shews himself in other ways, but here as fire. When the water of Gangâ rises, a Goddess is there; in Svarga she shows herself differently, but here as a rushing stream. If you cannot believe this, the "Mahâbhârata" will always puzzle you; for it relates things as they really happened, instead of in the way in which they look to our eyes. Instead of saying the fire burned the forest of Khâṇḍava, it says Agni burned it. It talks always of what the Gods are doing, and people who do not believe in the Gods think that that is a fanciful way of putting things. Few people believe that such things happen now, and yet they do happen as much as ever they did. In other ages the God would often shew himself at work and let people see him. Now the Gods hide themselves, because the people have become materialistic and do not care for them. Now and then a person who is pure and loving sees them as in the old days, and such a person believes in a book like this, and its stories do not seem strange to him.

Men now often speak of the invisible side of nature as "supernatural." That is a mistake. The greater part of nature is made up of the worlds and the beings that are invisible to our physical senses, but who move this lower world.

In the old days the Gods taught men, sometimes directly, sometimes through great men called Sages, or Rishis. Mantras—that is, a word, or a sentence, of which the sound has power in the invisible worlds–were given to men to use, and great effects were produced by these mantras. Men were taught how to think, so that their thought had power. We read how a man thought of a God, and the God appeared. How he thought of a weapon, and the weapon came to him. Thought has the same power now, and scientific men are beginning to make experiments with it. Everyone could not use it in the old days to call a God, or a weapon, but only great men could use it, who had been taught by the Gods. Now-a-days some Yogîs can use thought in this way, for the Gods have not changed, nor have they changed their laws; it is only men who have grown weak, because they are unbelieving.

The Gods guide the world. As a coachman guides his horses, so the Gods guide the world. As you might sit in a carriage and pull the reins this way and that, the horses obediently moving the carriage, so the Gods sit over the world and pull the forces one way or the other, and then the world is moved. They are always trying to drive the world the best way. The world is making a long journey, and there are many side-roads off the main track. We call the main track "evolution", the way of the world from the beginning to the end of it. If you go from here (Benares) to Allahabad, you pass many side-roads, but going along the trunk road you reach Allahabad in the shortest time. The Gods drive the world along the trunk road, evolution, but men often want to turn down side-roads that look pleasant. But the Gods have dug ditches and put up sign-posts along the main road, and, when men wilfully try to leave it, they fall into the ditches and knock up against the posts, and then we say they are suffering pain and trouble. But these pains and troubles are the very best things that can happen to them, for if the Gods had not made the wrong ways full of pain, men would wander away and lose themselves.

Sometimes a whole nation goes wrong. Then the Gods place in its way a great war, or a famine, or a plague. The nation is going wrong and must be driven right, or has gone wrong and must suffer, so as not to go wrong again. And the Great War, the story of which we are going to study, was brought about by the Gods, because it was necessary for the evolution of the nation. We see many men and animals killed in a war, and say: "How terrible! how shocking." But men and animals are only killed when the bodies they are in are of no more use: when a man cannot do any more in a particular body, the Gods strike it away, so that the man may have a better one. We call this "death". The body is like a coat that we wear, and when we outgrow it, it is torn up. Instead of regarding a God as cruel when he strikes away a body, you should think of him as kind, setting the man free to grow. Many of the men who were killed in this Great War went from their bodies to sit in Svarga with the Gods.

The work of the Gods is to carry out the law of the Supreme Lord, or Íshwara, who is manifested to us as a Trinity, Mahâdeva, Vishṇu and Brahmâ. This law is that the universe shall evolve into an image of God, and the Gods work for that end, and not for furthering separate personal aims. This makes their duties different from the duties of men. They have to test people; so they put difficulties and temptations and trials in their way, in order that men may grow strong, and learn wisdom and gain virtue. In this work they must often do things that men ought not to do, and they are not examples for men in conduct, any more than a king, or judge, or magistrate, in punishing a man who has committed a crime, is an example that you are to follow. If a man steals your shoes, the magistrate puts him in prison for breaking the law, though he has stolen nothing from the magistrate and the magistrate is not angry. But if you, from whom he has stolen the shoes, get angry and lock him up and keep him as a prisoner, you would be doing wrong. When you are older you will learn that all things that are wrong are wrong because they are done from what is called "a personal motive"—that is, from thinking and acting in your own way to please yourself, instead of doing the will of God.

We also learn from the "Mahâbhârata' that when a nation goes wrong, it suffers. This is what we call a moral law, and this law is worked out by the Gods. If India is to become rich, strong and free, as she once was, it can only be by Indians becoming pure and religious and good. There is no other way. For the Gods rule the world, and they make national greatness the reward of doing right, because that is the law. If people do wrong, the great nation becomes small, and the small nation that does right grows great.

When the time comes for a vast change in the life of a nation—as it came in India 5,000 years ago—great men are born into that nation. Some of these men are great in goodness, some are great in evil—strong, bad, men. These men are born because they are wanted in the nation, and they are men who have prepared themselves in past lives for important work. These great men, good and bad, are not here for the first time. In former lives the good ones had grown good and strong, till they were fit to be born at a critical time to work with the Gods. Others, the bad ones, had been selfish, cruel, revengeful, and they had fitted themselves to resist the good law of evolution, and by their resistance to bring on troubles that would teach the nation it was going wrong.

Both the good and the bad men had made their own fates, one set to work with the Gods, the other set to work against them. There is no favoritism on the part of the Gods, but suitable men are guided to the places they have earned, and are born in them.

We are told in the Ádi Parva, the first volume, of the "Mahâbhârata", about the preparations that were made in Svarga for the Great War. The Gods consulted, and decided that certain men should be born as leaders; four men were chosen, who in the past had filled the office of king of the Gods; the king of the Gods is called Indra, and these four men had all been Indras. The present Indra had one day behaved proudly, and had been condemned by Mahâdeva to lose his power for awhile. "Those that are of disposition like thine," said Mahâdeva, "never obtain my grace." And He went on to say that he and four other Indras should be born as men, and perform a certain task, and then return to Svarga. Then four of these Indras prayed that they might have divine fathers when they were born of women, and the fifth Indra said that he would create from himself the fifth man who was to fulfil the task. To this Mahâdeva agreed. (Ádi Parva, § 199.) When the time came, the four Indras were born as Yudhisṭhira, and Bhîma, and the twins Nakula and Sahadeva, the Gods Dharma (Justice), Vâyu (wind), and the twin Ashvins being their fathers; and Arjuna—who had been Nara, a great Rishi—was born as the son of the present Indra. And these were the five mighty warriors whose deeds we are going to study, and who were the conquerors in the Great War.

And as a new age was to begin after the war, even the great God Vishṇu Himself took Avatâra as Shrî Krishṇa, accompanied by Shesha, the eternal serpent, as His brother Balarâma. (Âdi Parva, § 199.) An Avatâra is a special manifestation of the Supreme Being in a physical form, appearing in order to destroy evil, when it has become so strong that it threatens to stop evolution.

The "Mahâbhârata" contains the story of a race descended from a powerful king named Bharata. He was the son of Dushyanta and Shakuntalâ, whose story you must read some day. ("Shakuntalâ," a drama by Kâlîdâsa.) Bhârata means the descendants of Bharata, and mahâ means great. So our book is "The great story of the descendants of Bharata". One of these descendants was named Kuru, and he was a king who was also an ascetic. He carried out many austere practices in a field that was named after him Kurukshetra, or the field of Kuru, and it was on that field that the great battle took place. Among the descendants of Kuru were three brothers: the blind king Dhritarâshṭra, whose sons fought on the wrong side in the Great War; Pâṇḍu, the nominal father of the five princes who fought on the right side; and Vidura, a very wise and just man, holding high office in the kingdom. The story of the lives and deeds of these men is told in this great poem of eighteen volumes, or Parvas. Each Parva takes its name from the part of the story told in it.

This poem was recited to a number of ascetics, resting themselves in the forest of Naimisha, by Agrashravâ, the son of Lomaharshaṇa, surnamed Sauti. One of these Rishis asked him whence he had come, and he answered that he had come from attending a great sacrifice, the Snake-Sacrifice of king Janamejaya. There he had heard recited the poem called the "Mahâbhârata," and he had himself learned it. It was composed by a famous Sage, named Krishṇa Dvaipâyana Veda Vyâsa—Krishṇa, because he was so dark; Dvaipâyana, because he was born on an island; Veda Vyâsa, because he had divided, i. e. compiled and arranged, the Vedas. The Rishis asked Sauti to recite the poem to them, and he did so. That is the story which we shall begin to study in the next chapter.

CHAPTER II.

THE YOUTH OF THE HEROES

We must now begin our story of the Great War by studying some of the events recorded in the Ádi Parva, the first volume, of the "Mahâbhârata". We shall learn something about the youth of the heroes of the story, and something about their parents, their circumstances and their education. Further we shall see, in studying these, the working of some of the great principles spoken of in the Introduction.

Bhîshma is the greatest and most heroic figure in this story; he is one of the noblest men of the Áryan race, a perfect example of conduct for men living in the world. He never falls into any of the sins into which most men fall; all through his life he does the right thing at the right time; he never loses his balance; he is never exaggerated; he keeps on the middle line of duty, neither leaning to the right nor to the left. He is a teacher and a counsellor; he is perfect as son, as guardian, as statesman. In every part of his life he does his duty.

Long before Bhîshma was born, there was a great festival among the Gods, and a king named Mahâbhisha, who had reached heaven by his sacrifices, was present at this festival. Gangâ, the queen of rivers, was also there, and the wind blew aside her clothes, exposing her bosom; the Gods bent their heads, so that she might not feel confused, but not so king Mahâbhisha. Then Brahmâ pronounced a curse on the king; that is, He foretold the suffering which he had brought on himself in the future by his wrong thought and act. [The future results of our thoughts and acts are called our "karma", and a "curse" from a God or a Rishi is a foretelling of this karma.] This king having acted against modesty, Brahmâ said that he must be re-born on earth instead of remaining in heaven; "Gangâ too will be born in the world of men and will inflict injuries on thee. But when thy anger is provoked, then thou shalt be freed from my curse."

The time came for the rebirth of Mahâbhisha, and he was born as the son of Pratîpa, a very pious king. One day, when the latter was engaged in ascetic practices, the Goddess Gangâ took the form of a lovely maiden, and, seating herself on his lap, begged him to marry her. King Pratîpa refused, but promised to marry her to his son. She accepted his offer, but warned him that his son would not be able to judge whether her acts were proper or improper. The king then, with his wife, performed austerities (underwent many bodily hardships), that he might have a noble son, and Mahâbhisha took birth as his child, being named Shâṇtanu, the son of the Peaceful, because his father had controlled his passions. When Shântanu had grown into a youth, his father said to him that a celestial maiden had once come to him, and that she would seek Shântanu as her husband; when she comes, said the father, "accept her as thy wife. And, O sinless one, judge not of the propriety of anything she does, and ask not who she is, or whose, or whence, but accept her as thy wife at my command." Then Shântanu was crowned king by his father—who took to the ascetic life—and he reigned happily. One day, wandering along the banks of Gangâ, he saw a lovely maiden, and, falling in love with her, begged her to become his wife. The maiden, who was none other than the Goddess Gangâ herself, consented to marry him, but told him that he must never interfere with her actions: "Nor must thou ever address me unkindly. As long as thou shalt behave kindly, I promise to live with thee. But I shall certainly leave thee the moment thou interferest with me, or speakest to me an unkind word." The king answered, "Be it so," and they were married, and lived very happily together. Presently a child was born, and the queen took the child and threw it into the river, saying, "This is for thy good." The same thing happened with the second child, and with the third and fourth, up to the seventh. And the poor king grew very troubled and unhappy. He "could not approve of such conduct," says the story-teller. "But he said not a word, lest his wife should leave him. But when the eighth child was born, and his wife, as before, was about to throw it smilingly into the river, the king, with a sorrowful countenance, and desirous of saving it from destruction, addressed her and said: "Slay it not! who art thou and whose? why dost thou slay thine own children? Murderess of thy sons, the load of thy sins is great."

Poor king Shântanu! the trial was a very severe one, and he forgot his father's command. His wife answered: "I shall not slay this child of thine. But according to our agreement, the period of my stay with thee is at an end. I am Gangâ, the daughter of Jahnu." Then she explained to him that the eight Vasus, celestial beings, had, a long time before, stolen away from a great Rishi the cow of plenty, Nandini, one of them, named Dyau, being the actual thief. The Rishi was very displeased, and declared that the Vasus should be born upon earth, as the result of their sin. They begged his pardon very humbly, so the Rishi said that they should be set free again from human life within a year of their births, with the exception of Dyau, who, "for his sinful act, shall have to dwell on earth for a long time." Then the Vasus went to Gangâ, and begged her, when she became a woman, to let them be born as her children, praying her to throw them into the water as soon as they were born, and thus to free them from the physical body of punishment. "I did as they desired," concluded the Goddess, "in order to free them from their earthly life. And, O best of kings, because of the Rishi's curse, this one only, Dyau himself, is to live for some time on earth." Then the Goddess disappeared, taking with her the eighth child, the Vasu Dyau, afterwards named Devavrata. [§ 96-99.]

People are often very much afraid of dying. But you see when a God is born here, he feels as if he were put into prison, and looks on death as a friend who opens the gate of the prison. Down here we rejoice when a child is born, and we weep when a person dies. It is as if people made a festival when a friend is put into jail, and wept when he is set free. In every death, it is a God who sets free the soul, just as Gangâ set free the Vasus. Only, this story shows us the Gods at work, so that we may learn to see their kind hands, in all the things that make us sorry because we do not understand.

Gangâ took away her son, as we have seen, but, when he had grown to be a youth, she brought him to his father, trained in knowledge and the use of arms; and in "all branches of learning, spiritual and worldly, his skill was very great. His strength and energy were extraordinary." And his filial piety was as great as his knowledge. This he shewed in a very striking way. One day his father was wandering on the banks of the Yamunâ, and saw a lovely girl whom he desired to make his wife. She was only a fisherman's daughter, but the fisherman would not give her to the king unless he would promise that the son born of her should inherit the throne. This the king would not do, as he would not put aside the son he already had, and he returned home very sad. Devavrata lovingly enquired the reason for his father's grief, and as his father would not tell him, he went for advice to an old minister, devoted to the king. This minister told him about the fisherman's daughter, and Devavrata went, with a noble escort of warrior chiefs, to ask the fisherman to give his daughter as wife to the king The fisherman said that he could not give the maiden Satyavatî to the king, because the king had a son who would be the rival of any son of Satyavatî. Then Devavrata said before all the chiefs: "Listen to my vow. I will do all you wish. The son that may be born of this maiden shall be our king." Thus he threw away the crown, that he might gratify his father's wish. Still the fisherman was not content, but said that while he felt sure Devavrata would keep his promise, he had some doubts whether his children would keep it as well.* Then spoke out Devavrata: "I have first relinquished my right to the throne. I shall now settle the question of my children. O fisherman! from this day I adopt the vow of Brahmacharya [celibacy]. Though I die sonless, I shall yet attain to regions of perpetual bliss in heaven." Then flowers rained down from the sky on the son who sacrificed himself to please his father, and divine voices cried out: "This is Bhîshma!" (the Terrible.) Yes! this was Bhîshma, beginning a stainless life of duty by renouncing what men hold most dear. And turning to the maiden, he said sweetly: "O mother, ascend this chariot and let us go home." So he brought her to his father, who blessed him, saying: "Death shall never come to thee as long as thou desirest to live. Truly, death shall only approach thee, O sinless one, having first obtained thy leave." [§ 100.]

King Shântanu died, leaving two sons, and Bhîshma became their protector, placing the elder, Chitrângada, on the throne. Chitrângada fell in battle, and his younger brother Vichitravîrya, still a youth, became king, and it was necessary to find him a wife. At that time, king's daughters were often won in marriage at what was called a Svayamvara, a "self-choice." Many kings assembled and took part in games, feats of strength, and fights, and, out of them all, the princess chose as her husband the one who was most successful and pleased her best. She showed her choice by throwing a garland of flowers round the neck of the chosen. Vichitravîrya, being only a youth, could not enter into such a contest, so Bhîshma, who was ruling the kingdom under the queen-mother, went in his stead. There were three princesses, sisters, and Bhîshma quietly took them up on his chariot, and, addressing all the kings, reminded them of the custom that a maiden, at a Svayamvara, might be carried off by force, the captor fighting all his rivals for her possession. "Ye monarchs! I bear away these maidens by force. Strive ye, to the best of your might, to vanquish me or be vanquished!" A great fight followed, in which Bhîshma, single-handed, fought all the assembled kings and carried off the maidens in triumph, bringing "the daughters of the king of Kâshî unto the Kurus as tenderly as if they were his daughters-in-law, or younger sisters, or daughters." The eldest princess, however, told him that in her heart she had chosen another king as her husband, and he yielded to her wish, marrying the two other sisters, Ambikâ and Ambâlikâ, to his young brother. The youth, however, died, leaving no children, and that greatest of misfortunes to a kingly race, the extinction of the family, threatened the line of Shântanu. [§ 102.]

Satyavatî, broken-hearted, implored Bhîshma to take the throne and to marry the widowed princesses. Friends and relatives begged him to do as the queen wished, and again throne and family joys were placed within his reach. Only his vow stood between him and the crown with wedded happiness. Only his vow! But to Bhîshma truth was more than anything the world could give. Read his answer, all Hindu boys, that you may understand what kind of men once made India great. "O mother! what thou sayest is certainly sanctioned by virtue. But thou knowest what my vow is in the matter of begetting children. Thou knowest also all that happened in connection with thy dower. O Satyavatî! I repeat the pledge I once gave. I would renounce the three worlds, the empire of heaven, or anything that may be greater than that, but truth I will never renounce. Earth may renounce its scent, water may renounce its moisture, light may renounce its power of showing forms, the air may renounce its perceptibility to touch, the sun may renounce his glory, fire his heat, the moon his cool rays, space its capacity to generate sound, the slayer of Vitra his prowess, the God of justice his impartiality, but I renounce not truth!"

The weeping Satyavatî still urged her plea, but Bhîshma could not be moved. "O Queen! take not thine eyes from virtue. Oh! destroy us not. Breach of truth in a Kshattriya is never applauded in our religious books. I shall soon tell thee, O Queen, what is the established Kshattriya usage to which recourse may be had to prevent Shântanu's line from becoming extinct upon earth. Hearing me, reflect on what should be done, consulting learned priests and those that are acquainted with practices allowable in times of emergency and distress, forgetting not at the same time what is the ordinary course of social conduct." [§ 103.]

Bhîshma then advised that some great Rishi should be asked to be the father of children who, being borne by the two widows, would be regarded as the sons of the dead man. Satyavatî told him that there was a Rishi, who had been born of her with Parâshara as his father, and who, having been a mighty ascetic in the past, had gone away with his father immediately after his rebirth. This was Krishṇa Dvaipâyana Vyâsa. He had promised his mother that he would come to her if she thought of him when she was in a difficulty. "I will now recollect him, if thou, O Bhîshma of mighty arms, so desirest." She then thought of the Rishi, and, on his coming, the difficulty was laid before him and his help was asked. He consented, and even gave up the year of purification that he at first imposed on the princesses, saying: "If I am to give unto my brother children so unseasonably, then let the ladies bear my ugliness. That of itself shall, in their case, be the austerest of penances." With great difficulty Satyavatî won her daughters-in-law to consent, for the sake of the family, to receive the great Rishi. But the elder princess, "seeing his dark visage, his matted locks of copper hue, his blazing eyes, his grim beard, closed her eyes in fear," and would not open them while he was there. Hence she drew to her, for her son, a soul whose karma it was to live in a blind body, and Vyâsa foretold that her son would be blind. This child was Dhritarâshṭra, who became the blind king of the Kurus. The second princess, Ambâlikâ, "beholding the Rishi, became pale with fear;" hence her son, born with a pale complexion, was named Pâṇḍu, the Pale; he was the father of the famous Pâṇḍavas, the five heroic brothers who were the conquerors in the Great War. A third child was desired by the queen, but Ambikâ refused to do her mother-in-law's bidding, and sent her maid, a Shûdra woman, to the Rishi instead; she, thinking of his spiritual greatness instead of his ugly body, behaved to him with deep respect and sweetness, and the Rishi blessed her, and the God of Justice was born to her as a son, and was named Vidura. These were the three brothers, Dhritarâshṭra, Pâṇḍu and Vidura, who played so prominent a part in the Great War—two of them being the fathers of the opposed princes, and Vidura, the third, the wise councillor of the blind king. [§ 104-106.]

Bhîshma took charge of the three boys and brought them up as if they were his own children. "And the children, having passed through the usual rites of their order, devoted themselves to vows and study. And they grew up into fine youths, skilled in the Vedas and in all athletic sports. And they became well skilled in exercises of the bow, in horsemanship, in encounters with the mace, sword and shield, in the management of elephants in battle, and the science of morality. Well read in history, and the Purâṇas, and various branches of learning, and acquainted with the truths of the Vedas and their branches, the knowledge they acquired was versatile and deep." You see that, in those days, a boy was taught to be religious and moral at the same time that he was trained to be athletic and skilful. [§ 109.]

Pânḍu was made king, as the eldest brother, Dhritarâshṭra, was blind. By the advice of Bhîshma, Dhritarâshṭra was married to Gândhârî, the daughter of the king of Suvala, and the sister of Shakuni, who later brought so much trouble into the family. There is a pretty story told of Gândhârî: when she heard that her future husband was blind, she bandaged her own eyes with a piece of cloth, wishing to share her husband's trouble and not to enjoy what he could not have. [§ 110.] Indian wives have always been remarkable for their devotion to their husbands.

As the wife of Pânḍu, Bhîshma desired Prithâ, the daughter of Shura, king of the Yâdavas. She was the sister of Vasudeva, who became the father of Shrî Krishṇa. At her Svayamvara she chose Pânḍu, thus fulfilling Bhîshma's wish, and a little later Bhîshma obtained for Pânḍu a second wife, Mâdrî, the sister of Shalya, the king of Mâdra. When a month had passed after the second marriage, king Pânḍu went out and conquered various kingdoms, bringing back to his capital, Hastinâpura, much spoil and animals of all kinds. He then went to the woods for the chase, and lived there awhile with his two wives. [§ 111-114.]

One day when Pâṇḍu was out hunting, he committed a very cruel act, shooting a stag that was coupling with its mate. This disregard of kindness brought on him the curse that if he sought to live as a husband with his wife he should immediately die. This sad sentence made the king very unhappy, as it meant that he would have to die childless. He gave away all his personal property and went to wander in the woods as an ascetic, his wives Prithâ, usually called Kuntî from the name of her adopted father, and Mâdrî, following him. [§ 118, 119.]

Now Pâṇḍu began, after a time, to long very much to have sons, and he consulted Kuntî how this might be brought about. She told him that, as a girl, she had very much pleased the great Rishi Durvâsâ by her services, and he had taught her a mantra by which she could call on any of the Gods to give her children. She asked her husband if she should now use this mantra, and thus obtain children from the Gods. He ordered her to call the God of Justice, Dharma and to ask him to give her a son. Thus was born Yudhishṭhira. And then Kuntî called on the strong God of Wind, Vâyu, and he gave her Bhîma. Then she invoked the king of the Gods, Indra, and he gave her Arjuna. Further, at the request of Pâṇḍu, Kuntî taught Mâdrî the mantra, and Mâdrî called the twin

Ashvins, who gave her the twins Nakula and Sahadeva. Now these are the five Pâṇḍavas, or sons of Pâṇḍu, given him by the Gods, and, as we saw in the Introduction, four of them had been Indras in the past, and were re-born with Gods for their fathers, while Arjuna was the great Rishi Nara, who took birth as the son of the present Indra.

One day, king Pâṇḍu forgot his vow, and sought the embraces of Mâdrî, who tried in vain to resist him, and as he touched her he died. The wife lay weeping, and was found by Kuntî beside their dead husband. Then arose a loving quarrel between the two wives, each of whom longed to die with Pâṇḍu; it was decided that Mâdrî should have that privilege as he had died in her arms, and she yielded up her breath, giving her two children into the care of Kuntî, who cherished them as if they were her own, making no difference between them and her three sons. A number of Rishis quickly came and conducted Kuntî and the five boys to Hastinâpura, to place them under the care of Dhritarâshṭra and Bhîshma. And the funeral rites and Shrâddha ceremonies were there duly celebrated. [§ 120-127.]

Meanwhile, king Dhritarâshṭra had a hundred sons and one daughter borne to him by his wife Gândhârî, through a special blessing bestowed on her.

The eldest of these, Duryodhana, had been born on the same day as Bhîma, but his birth was surrounded by the worst omens. There were storms and fires, and vultures and jackals and other low kinds of animals screamed and howled. For when men and nature are living harmoniously, nature shews sympathy with the course of human affairs, and bewails the coming of sorrow to the human race. This new-born child was to be the destroyer of his family and his country, and nature mourned over his coming. The wise Vidura indeed advised that he should be cast off by his family, but Dhritarâshṭra could not find it in his heart to abandon his son. So he kept him to his sorrow and his own undoing, forgetting that he was a king with a duty to his nation, as well as a father. [§ 115.]

Duryodhana was born at this time to serve the purposes of the Gods in the great object lesson that had to be given to the world, having prepared himself for such a career by the character he had made in his previous lives. He was strong and very brave, religious in many things, and doing much of his duty as a prince. But he was selfish. "I want to be first, I want to be king, I want everything my own way." These were his feelings, and he became miserable with jealousy when any one did better than he. That was the fault which brought him to ruin. For Yudhishṭhira being older than Duryodhana, the succession to the throne was his, though Duryodhana had been brought up as heir to the crown.

The Pâṇḍavas and the sons of Dhritarâshṭra now became companions, and the great strength of Bhîma—exerted in childish mischief—began to make trouble. He would knock the others down, hold ten of them under water all together till they were nearly drowned, shake a tree on which some of them had climbed till "down came the fruits and the fruit-pluckers at the same time." And though it is said that he tormented "them in childishness but not from malice," we cannot wonder that they did not like such rough play. Strong boys often make enemies by using their strength thoughtlessly. Duryodhana became very jealous of Bhîma's strength and determined to kill him. So he had built a pleasant summer-house on the banks of the Gangâ, and invited the Pâṇḍavas to a feast. At the feast, pretending to be very friendly, he gave Bhîma food with his own hands, having previously had the food poisoned. After the meal the boys played in the water, and Bhîma, feeling the effects of the poison, lay down on the ground when the others went into the summer-house to rest. Duryodhana stayed behind, and, when

Bhîma became insensible, he tied round him some trails of creepers and threw him into the water. Bhîma sank down till he reached the kingdom of the great snakes called Nâgas, and they bit him severely with their poison-fangs. But the snake-poison neutralised the vegetable poison in the food, and Bhîma recovered his senses. He burst his bonds and began killing the snakes, who called on their king Vâsukî to protect them. One of the serpents had been an ancestor of Bhîma through his mother, and at his request the king allowed Bhîma to drink some of his nectar, which gave immense strength. Eight days afterwards Bhîma returned home to his mother and brothers, who were very anxious about him, and told them what Duryodhana had done. But, by the advice of Vidura and Yudhishṭhira, no complaint was made against Duryodhana, even when he continued to plot against Bhîma and his brothers; yet, in spite of this kindness, his enmity towards the Pâṇḍavas continually grew.

"Meanwhile, the king, beholding the Kuru princes passing their time in idleness and growing naughty," as idle boys will, placed them under a tutor, named Kripa, to learn the use of arms. There was living in the house of Kripa, just then, a Brâhmaṇa named Droṇa, who was the husband of Kripa's sister. Droṇa was the son of a great sage, named Bharadvâja, and had had, as his fellow-student and playmate in his father's hermitage, the son of king Prishata, by name Drupada. Droṇa became versed in the science of arms, and further obtained from the great son of Bhrigu all his weapons and the mysteries of controlling them. Leaving the son of Bhrigu, he went to his old friend Drupada, then king of the Pânchâlas, and eagerly addressed him as his "friend." Drupada, very proud of his wealth and power, answered rudely that "kings can never be friends" with poor men, "and one who is not a king can never have a king for his friend"—words that were to bring trouble on him later. Droṇa went away without saying anything, and going to Hastinâpura, lived awhile with his brother-in-law, Kripa; while his mighty son, named Ashvatthâmâ, helped Kripa in teaching the princes. [§ 128, 129, 131, 132.]

One day, as the boys were playing ball, the ball fell into a dry well, and they could not recover it. A Brâhmaṇa was passing by, and they cried to him to get it out for them. He threw in his ring after it, and then, with some blades of grass, he brought up the ball. He also recovered his ring by shooting an arrow into it, and recalling the arrow. The boys, much surprised, were eager to do him some service, and he sent them to tell their story to Bhîshma. Now Bhîshma had been looking for a suitable tutor for the young princes, and, guessing that this wonderful Brâhmaṇa was no other than Droṇa, he went to him at once and brought him to the palace. Droṇa told his story, and Bhîshma begged him to take the princes as his pupils, rejoicing over obtaining such a tutor. [§ 133.]

When the boys came to him, Droṇa told them that he had a purpose in his heart, and asked them to promise that, when they had learned the science of arms, they would carry it out. The rest remained silent, but Arjuna promised to do it, whatever it might be, and all through his pupilage he showed this ready devotion to his teacher, so that he became his favourite pupil. One evening, when Arjuna was taking his food, the wind blew out the lamp, and he went on "eating in the dark, his hand, from habit, going to his mouth. His attention being thus called to the force of habit, the strong-armed son of Pâṇḍu set his heart upon practising with his bow in the night." This energy of his much pleased his teacher. By observing small things, as Arjuna did, you can often learn what is useful.

Many princes came to Droṇa, eager to become his pupils, and among them a prince named Ekalavya son of the king of the Nishâdas, a very low tribe. Droṇa refused to take Ekalavya as his pupil, as he might only teach the science of arms—which included the use of mantras and the control of thought—to those who by their lives had earned the reward of being born into the higher castes. Ekalavya was not angry at this repulse, but touching Droṇa's feet reverently, he went to the forest. There he made a clay image of Droṇa, worshipping it as his teacher, and practised before it the use of arms. He gained great skill by his reverence for the teacher and his devotion to his purpose, and one day, when the princes were in the wood, he astonished them with a striking proof of his mastery of the bow. The princes related to Droṇa what they had seen, and Droṇa went with Arjuna to the wood. Ekalavya, seeing him coming, went to meet him and touched his feet, and then stood before him, respectfully waiting for his commands. Then said Droṇa: "If, O hero, thou art really my pupil, give me then my fee." Then Ekalavya offered to give him anything he possessed, "for there is nothing that I may not give unto my preceptor." "Ekalavya," answered Droṇa, "if thou art really intent on making me a gift, I should like then to have the thumb of thy right hand." "Hearing these cruel words of Droṇa, who had asked of him his thumb as tuition-fee, Ekalavya, ever devoted to truth and desirous also of keeping his promise, with a cheerful face and an unafflicted heart, cut off without ado his thumb, and gave it unto Droṇa."

You may think it was a hard and cruel demand that Droṇa made, but a very important lesson underlies it. A man is born according to his past thoughts and actions, and his body is part of his karma. He must not forcibly snatch at advantages denied to him by his physical condition, but must patiently wear his disabilities till he has worn them out, and the way opens before him. Ekalavya would not wait. He resolutely grasped the fruit that to him was forbidden, and the body that had sinned had to pay its debt. But the love for his teacher with which his young heart was filled, his patience, his resolute will—all these were working for him on the higher planes, and assuring to him a future of success even in the physical world.

One day Droṇa wished to test his pupils, so he placed an artificial bird in a tree and called them to shoot at it in turn. First Yudhishṭhira took up his bow, and, pointing out the bird, Droṇa asked him: "What dost thou see, O prince? Seest thou the tree, myself, or thy brothers?" Then Yudhishṭhira answered that he saw them all. "Stand thou apart," said

Droṇa. "It is not for thee to strike the aim." The same thing happened with each of the princes in turn, until Arjuna was called. Droṇa repeated his question, and Arjuna replied: "I see the bird only, but not the tree or thyself." Quietly answered Droṇa: "If thou seest the vulture, then describe it to me." "I see only the head of the vulture, not its body," said the steadily attentive Arjuna. "Shoot," said Droṇa, delighted. [§ 134]

Close attention: there is one of the qualities we all want to cultivate. If you are to aim at one thing, and you see five or six others at the same time, your aim will not be steady. You must fix your mind on the thing you are going to do. If you are learning Arithmetic, do not see what is going on outside the room, or what the boy next you is doing; fix your thought on the sum your teacher is working out on the black board, and see nothing else.

At last the princes' education was finished, and it was decided to give a great exhibition of their skill. So all the court and the citizens came together to see the feats of arms. Arjuna excelled all the others; and it may interest you to know that one of the sports was to shoot at a moving iron boar; he shot five arrows together from his bowstring into the mouth of this boar. Just as the exhibition was over a great noise was heard, and the crowd made way for a young warrior, named Karṇa, of whom we shall hear much as the story goes on. He also had been a pupil of Droṇa, and had always shown much jealousy towards Arjuna. He now challenged Arjuna by repeating all his feats, after which the two advanced to meet each other in single combat. Then Kripa, according to rule, proclaimed the name and family of Arjuna, and asked for the lineage of his challenger that it also might be proclaimed. Karṇa turned pale, and Duryodhana hastily interposed, saying that if royalty were a necessary condition for meeting Arjuna in a duel, he would make Karṇa a king. Karṇa was then crowned king of Anga, and swore friendship to Duryodhana, who had given him a kingdom. Just then an old charioteer tottered into the lists, and Karṇa, going to meet him, bowed at his feet, and was addressed by him as his son. At this, Bhîma sprang up angrily, and mockingly addressing Karṇa as the son of a charioteer, declared him unfit to fight with the royal Arjuna. Up leapt Duryodhana in wrath, passionately defending his friend, but just then the sun went down and the meeting dispersed, leaving the question undecided as to the relative prowess of Arjuna and Karṇa. This question, strangely enough, was never set at rest.

Now had the time come to pay Droṇa his fee as preceptor, and calling his pupils—ready to go forth into the world—Droṇa said: "Seize Drupada, the king of Pânchâla, in battle and bring him unto me. That shall be the most acceptable fee." Then the princes went forth, the Kurus and the Pâṇḍavas, and fought against Drupada; the Kurus were dispersed by the valour of Drupada, but Arjuna with his brothers carried all before them, and finally seized Drupada himself and bore him away captive to Droṇa. Droṇa then spoke to his conquered foe, and instead of speaking bitterly, his words were sweet. "Fear not for thy life, though it dependeth now on the will of thy foe. Dost thou now desire to revive thy friendship with me?" Smiling, he went on: "Fear not for thy life, brave king. We Brâhmaṇas are ever forgiving. And, O bull among Kshattriyas, my affection and love for thee have grown with my growth in consequence of our having sported together in childhood in the hermitage. Therefore, O king, I ask for thy friendship again. And as a boon, I give thee back half thy kingdom. Thou toldest me before that none who was not a king could be a king's friend. Therefore is it that I retain half thy kingdom. Thou art the king of all the territories lying on the southern side of the Bhâgirathî, while I become king of all the territory on the north of that river. And, O Pânchâla, if it pleaseth thee, know me from henceforth as thy friend."

Thus nobly did Droṇa repay the cruel insult he had received. [§ 135-140.]

—:o:—

CHAPTER III.

THE PERILS AND TRIUMPHS OF THE PÂṆḌAVAS

The time of youth being over, and the princes proved as gallant warriors, Dhritarâshṭra proclaimed Yudhishṭhira, the eldest brother, the heir to the crown. He thus installed him, it is written, "on account of his firmness, fortitude, patience, benevolence, frankness and unswerving honesty of heart. And within a short time Yudhishṭhira, the son of Kuntî, by his good behaviour, manners, and close application to business, overshadowed the deeds of his father." The other brothers devoted themselves to conquest, and extended the limits of the kingdom, but unfortunately their success made king Dhritarâshṭra very jealous of them, and "his sentiments towards the Pâṇḍavas became suddenly poisoned, and from that day the monarch became so anxious that he could not sleep." [§ 141.] The sons of Pâṇḍu were growing so rich, the people loved and praised them so much, and the four younger were so devoted to their eldest brother, that the blind king felt that he and his children were thrown quite into the shade. So he called one of his ministers, Kanika, and asked him what he should do and Kanika replied with a clever but cruel story. There was, once a jackal who lived in a wood with four friends—a tiger, a wolf, a mouse and a mongoose. One day, in order to catch a strong swift deer, the jackal advised that the mouse should nibble his feet while he was sleeping, and the tiger should pounce on him when he could not run. This was done, and the jackal offered to watch the deer while the others bathed. The tiger came back first, and the jackal told him that the mouse boasted he had slain the deer and that the tiger owed him his dinner. Then the pride of the tiger was roused, and he went away to get his own dinner. Next came the mouse, and the jackal frightened him away by telling him the mongoose would eat him. The wolf fled on hearing that the tiger was angry with him, and the mongoose retreated when the jackal told him that he had fought with and conquered the other three. Then the jackal happily feasted on the deer. So, said Kanika, should kings conquer their foes one by one, by arts that touched a weak spot. (§ 142.)

Now Duryodhana became much distressed by hearing the people praise Yudhishṭhira and desire him as their king; and he went to his father and complained that the crown would certainly pass to Pâṇḍu's line unless he took steps to prevent it. "Send them away," he begged his father; "banish, by some gentle means, the Pâṇḍavas to the town of Vâranâvarta, O king. When the sovereignty shall have been vested in me, then, O Bhârata, may Kuntî with her children come back from that place." The king could find no cause of quarrel against the Pâṇḍavas, so, pretending to wish to please them, he told them that they might go, if they liked, to see a religious festival in honour of Shiva that was being held at Vâranâvarta. They agreed, not wishing to go, but fearing to refuse. And now prince Duryodhana, with Karṇa, Dushâsana and Shakuni, made up a fiendish plot, and bribed a man named Purochana to build a palace at Vâranâvarta, making it of hemp, resin, lac, and other inflammable materials, purposing to set it on fire when the princes were settled there, so that they might be burned to death.

The people of Hastinâpura surrounded the princes on their departure in much distress, complaining that they should be sent away; but Yudhishṭhira bade them remember that "The king is our father, worthy of regard, our spiritual guide and our superior. To achieve with unsuspicious hearts whatever he biddeth is, indeed, our duty." He bade them go home quietly, and, as they went, Vidura spoke to him in the Mlechchha tongue—so that no one might understand—warning him against weapons not made of steel, and saying that a man might be safe from fire by making his house like that of the jackal (with many roads out), and might learn the way about by wandering. Yudhishṭhira understood, and when Purochana invited him to the costly house he had built, he accepted the invitation, but went out hunting daily that he might learn all the forest paths, and had a subterranean way secretly dug by a miner, sent by Vidura, from the chamber where he slept with his brothers to the forest outside.

For a year the princes lived in the house of lac, until Purochana thought the time had come for setting it on fire. But Bhîma was beforehand with him. Kuntî had been feeding a number of Brâhmaṇas one night; among these came a Nishâda women with her five sons, who, becoming intoxicated, remained when the rest went home. Of this Bhîma knew nothing; he only knew that Purochana was there. He set the house on fire in several places, and then he, his brothers and his mother ran out through the underground way to the forest. There they were met by a messenger from the good Vidura, who had a boat ready to carry them over the river Gangâ, and, crosstng the stream, they went southwards. Meanwhile ihe blazing house drew the people together, and they found the remains of Purochana and of a woman with five youths, and gathering these latter up, as the remains of the Pâṇḍavas and their mother, they carried them, weeping, to Dhritarâshṭra. Then the blind king and all the citizens wept and lamented, but "Vidura did not weep much because he knew the truth." (§ 143-152.)

The Pâṇḍavas were now fugitives, homeless wanderers, living in wild forests amid many hardships. It broke their hearts to see their mother sleeping on the bare ground, exposed to the weather, she on whom no wind had blown too roughly. Bhîma carried them all on his strong shoulders, and fought for them, and watched them while they slept. One night a Râkshasa, a giant, smelling human beings near, sent his sister to kill them and bring them to him for food; but she, seeing Bhîma look so splendid and strong as he watched over his sleeping mother and brothers, fell in love with him instead of trying to murder him. As she was telling Bhîma of his danger, the Râkshasa, Hidimva, came hurrying up very angry, crying that he would kill his sister with her new friends. "Stop, stop," said Bhîma, smiling at him; "do not awaken these people sleeping so comfortably;" but he was himself quite ready for a fight. So up he jumped as the giant ran at him, and, pulling him away to a distance so as not to awaken the sleepers, he began wrestling with him. That was indeed a fight: they pulled up trees and rocks and fought with them, and struggled up and down, till the brothers woke and called on Bhîma to finish the fight, and he tossed the great body of the Râkshasa up in the air, and, dashing it on the ground, broke his back, bending him double. Many such a fight was this strong Bhîma to wage, to clear the world of mighty and evil beings who made life impossible for quiet harmless folk. When there are many bad and powerful people oppressing the poor and the helpless, the Gods use a strong man like Bhîma to sweep off the earth those who make it unfit to live in. It was Bhîma's duty to fight hard against oppressors, and his great strength was meant to be used in defence of the weak.

After her brother's death, the Râkshasî, making herself into a beautiful woman, lived with Bhîma as his wife, and they had a giant son named Ghatotkacha, who was very useful later on to the Pâṇḍavas. Meanwhile the brothers lived by hunting, till they met Vyâsa, who told them to remain, awaiting his return, in the house of a Brâhmaṇa to whom he brought them. Then they used to beg for food as ascetics, and Kuntî would divide among them what they collected as alms, giving half to Bhîma, and sharing the second half among the four brothers and herself. One day, when the brothers except Bhîma, were out, Kuntî found the Brâhmaṇa weeping with his wife and his two children, and heard him lamenting that he or one of his dear ones must perish. Then the wife said that she was quite willing to die, and that her husband must sacrifice her for the good of all. And the daughter said that she was the one to die, for they would have to give her away in marriage and might as well give her to death. And the little son, too young to understand, said he would fight the wicked giant with a blade of grass. As they were smiling at the child, Kuntî asked what was the matter, and learned that to a Râkshasa was paid tribute consisting of a cart-load of rice and two buffaloes and the human being who took him the food. The householders paid this tribute in turn, and the turn of this Brâhmaṇa had come; he and his family were disputing who should take the food, and each wanted to be the victim and to save the others. Then Kuntî said cheerfully that one of her sons would take the food, and when the Brâhmaṇa said that he would never be so wicked as to send a guest to his death, she answered that Brâhmaṇas must always be protected, and that her son was strong and would be in no danger. Then she called Bhîma, who gladly undertook the task of saving their kind host. When Yudhishṭhira came home and heard what had happened, he became very anxious and gently reproached his mother for sending Bhîma into danger; but Kuntî said it was a good deed to reward their host and deliver the town, and that Bhîma should perform this virtuous action, such being the duty of the Kshattriya. So Bhîma went off, driving the bullocks with the rice, and when he reached the place where the giant lived, feeling a little hungry, he sat down and began to eat up the rice. Out came the giant and gave Bhîma a great blow on the back, but Bhîma smiled at him and went on with his dinner. Then the giant pulled up a tree and struck at him, but Bhîma caught the tree in his left hand and continued to eat. When Bhîma had quite finished, he washed himself, and then turned cheerfully to fight. Great was the struggle, but Bhîma won, and broke the Râkshasa's back across his knee. Then he went quietly back again, after telling the giant's relatives to give up the practice of eating men, and all the townsmen rejoiced that their terrible enemy was slain and that they could live in peace. [§135-166.]

Now one day a Brâhmaṇa came as a guest to the house where the Pâṇḍavas were staying, and told the princes the story of Droṇa and Drupada, and spoke of the grief that Drupada had felt when he had been conquered and left with only half his kingdom. He was always longing for a son who might conquer Droṇa, and at last he performed a great sacrifice to obtain such a son. At the sacrifice, the priest called Drupada's queen to take the sanctified butter that she might bear a son and daughter, but she was not ready; so the priest poured the butter on the fire, and from the flames sprang forth a boy, crowned and armed, and a voice cried: "This prince has been born for the destruction of Droṇa." Then, as the people wondered, a lovely girl arose from the centre of the sacrificial platform, dark-complexioned, with dark curling hair, and again the voice cried: "This dark-complexioned girl will be the first of all women, and she will be the cause of the destruction of many Kshattriyas." And these were Dhrishtadyumna, who led the army of the Pâṇḍavas at Kurukshetra, and Krishṇâ the beautiful, who became the wife of the sons of Pâṇḍu. Then Droṇa, knowing the future, took the prince and taught him the use of all weapons, as a return for the half-kingdom of which he had deprived his father Drupada.

Now Vyâsa came to see the princes, and bade them go to the capital of Drupada, king of the Pânchâlas. He told them that, in her last birth, Krishṇâ, the daughter of Drupada, had prayed repeatedly to Mahâdeva for a husband, and He had told her that, as she had five times demanded a husband of Him, five husbands should she have in another life. She was the wife appointed for the Pânḍavas, and Vyâsa bade them go to Drupada's court. On the way, by the advice of a Gandharva, they visited an ascetic named Dhaumya, and prayed him to become their priest; and he, accepting them as his disciples, went with them to Panchâla. Further on they met some Brâhmaṇas, journeying to the same place to attend the Svayamvara of Krishṇâ, and, joining their company, supported themselves by begging like Brâhmaṇas.

Now Drupada—called also Yajnasena—had long desired that Arjuna should become the husband of his daughter, and, knowing his skill as an archer, he had made a great bow that he thought no one else could bend, and set up a mark high in the sky, proclaiming that he who could string the bow and hit the mark should marry his daughter. Great was the crowd of kings assembled to take part in the contest, and among them came as onlooker with His brother Valadeva, or Balarâma, Shrî Krishṇa, looking with eyes of love on Arjuna and his brothers, for the first time seeing in this birth His ancient friend.

Soon the struggle began, and prince after prince

took up the great bow and failed to string it, while Krishṇâ looked on with shining eyes, seeking her future lord. In all that great assembly none was found to bend the bow, till Karṇa sprang forward and seizing the bow, bent and strung it and fitted an arrow to the string. But as the sons of Pâṇḍu thought themselves lost, Krishṇâ's clear voice rang bell-like over the crowd: "I will not choose a Suta for my lord," and Karṇa cast away the bow and went. Then Arjuna stepped forward, looking like a Brâhmaṇa, a stripling still though grandly formed and tall, and he lifted the bow lightly and strung it without an effort, and, drawing it, sent the five arrows swiftly to the mark. Then flowers fell from the sky, and musicians and bards broke into music, and Krishṇâ, royally garbed and smiling, with flowers and water in a golden dish, approached Arjuna, and threw on him a white robe and a garland of sweet blossoms, thus showing that she chose him as her husband. Then he turned to leave the field, and she followed him meekly, who had won her and whom her heart approved. But there arose a great uproar among the kings, who cried, "This maiden is a Kshattriya and must not be given to a Brâhmaṇa!" and they crowded together to take her from Arjuna by force. Then Arjuna picked up the great bow, and Bhîma tore up a tree as weapon, and together the two brothers faced the rushing kings. Shalya was there and Duryodhana and Karṇa, and all men wondered when they saw the two apparent Brâhmaṇas hold their own against these warriors. And at last Shrî Krishṇa interposed and reminded the monarchs that Krishṇâ had been fairly won, and they left off fighting, and the brothers departed home to their mother.

As they came in, Kuntî was in the inner room, and they called out to her in play that they had brought home the day's alms; she answered, "Enjoy it, all of you," and then, seeing Krishṇâ, she exclaimed, "Oh! what have I said?" Yudhishṭhira had come back early, and the mother appealed to him to decide how she could avoid having uttered an untruth, and yet Krishṇâ be without sin. Arjuna had won her, let him marry her, said Yudhishṭhira. But Arjuna answered that he could not righteously marry before his two elder brothers. Then Yudhishṭhira remembered Vyâsa's strange prophecy, and said: "The auspicious Draupadî shall be the common wife of all." Just then in came Shrî Krishṇa, who said, touching the feet of His elder, Yudhishṭhira, "I am Krishṇa!" and they greeted each other joyfully, but soon parted, lest attention should be drawn to the sons of Pâṇḍu. Then, when they eaten, they lay down to sleep, the brothers lying side by side, their mother along their heads and Krishṇâ at their feet, and ere they slept they talked of weapons and battles as warriors would. Now Krishṇâ's brother, anxious about his sister's fate, had crept into the little house unseen, and overheard the conversation, and, hastening back to his father he told him that the youths were no Brâhmaṇas, nor were they Vaishyas nor Shûdras, for their talk was that of warriors, and they were like the sons of Pâṇḍu.

Then was Drupada glad exeedingly, and sent his priest to find out who these youths were; but Yudhishṭhira would only say that Krishṇâ had been fairly won, and that the king must not grieve that the princess should belong to the hero who had fulfilled the conditions he had himself laid down. Meanwhile the king prepared a feast, and gathered many things suitable to each of the four orders; and when the princes, after dining, turned to the weapons with eager interest, he was glad, hoping that they were Kshatriyas. At last he asked who they were, and Yudhishṭhira said that they were the sons of Pâṇḍu, and told the delighted king of their escape and later adventures.

Then came the question of Krishṇâ's marriage, and Drupada said that she might marry any one of the five brothers; but Yudhishṭhira said that his mother had ordered that Krishṇâ should be their common wife: we "ever enjoy equally a jewel we may obtain." But, protested Drupada, how may a woman have five husbands? "O son of Kunti, pure as thou art and acquainted with the rules of morality, it behoveth thee not to commit an act that is sinful, and opposed both to usage and the Vedas." "My tongue," said Yudhishṭhira, "never uttered an untruth. My heart also never turneth to that which is sinful. My mother commandeth so, and my heart also approveth of it." But king Drupada could not agree, and discussion arose, during which Vyâsa arrived and appeal was made to him. He took Drupada apart and told him that the five sons of Pâṇḍu were four Indras of the past and the son of the present Indra, and he showed him in a vision the divine forms of the brothers; then he explained that Krishṇâ was the Goddess Shrî, born as a woman in order that she might be the wife of these Indras, and that in her last birth Mahâdeva had decreed that she should thus have five husbands, because she had urgently asked five times over for a husband. On this Drupada yielded, and the princess Krishṇâ was married to the five sons of Pâṇḍu. [§ 167-200.]

The Pâṇḍavas now began to regain prosperity, Shrî Krishṇa sending them vast stores of wealth, but

Duryodhana and his friends, hearing of their escape, began fresh plots against them. Karṇa advised open war ere yet the Pâṇḍavas had grown strong, but Bhîshma declared that he could never approve of a quarrel with them, and that half the kingdom ought to be given over to them. "A good name," said he, "is, indeed, the source of one's strength......we, are fortunate that the Pâṇḍavas have not perished. We are fortunate that Kuntî liveth.........O tiger among men, hearing of the fate that overtook Kuntî, the world doth not regard Purochana as so guilty as it regardeth thee. O king, the escape, therefore, of the sons of Pâṇḍu with life from that conflagration, and their reappearance, do away with thy evil repute. Know, O thou of Kuru's race, that as long as those heroes live, the wielder of the thunder himself cannot deprive them of their ancestral share in the kingdom. The Pâṇḍavas are virtuous and united. They are being wrongly kept out of their equal share in the kingdom. If thou shouldst act rightly, if thou shouldst do what is agreeable to me, if thou shouldst seek the welfare of all, then give half the kindom unto them." Droṇa spoke in the same sense, as did Vidura, Karṇa bitterly opposing, and finally Dhritarâshṭra sent Vidura to bring the sons of Kuntî home.

Great was the joy of the people on their arrival; "the whole city became radiant," and king Dhritarâshṭra gave them half the kingdom, bidding them reside at Khâṇḍavaprastha. Khâṇḍavaprastha was at that time an unreclaimed desert, but the Pâṇḍavas soon built themselves a beautiful city on a site chosen with the help of Vyâsa. So fair was this city that men compared it with Indra's city, and called it Indraprastha.

One day Nârada came to see them, and, talking with the brothers, he warned them against the disunion that might arise from their having a common wife. He advised them to make some rule as to their relations with her, and they agreed that when one of them was in Krishṇâ's company, any one of the others that interrupted those two should go into the forest as an exile for twelve years. Now it happened that some robbers stole a Brâhmaṇa's cattle, and the man, lamenting his loss, cried to the Pâṇḍavas for justice. Arjuna heard him and promised to redress the wrong, but his weapons were all in the room where Yudhishṭhira was sitting with Draupadî. What could he do? If he did not protect the Brâhmaṇa blame would fall on the king, for a king in whose kingdom wrong went unpunished was held as sinful. True, if he went into the room he would incur the penalty of exile. "But I care not if I have to go to the woods and die there. Virtue is superior to the body, and lasteth after the body has perished." So he went into the room and spoke to Yudhishṭhira, and, taking his weapons, pursued the thieves and restored his cattle to the Brâhmaṇa. Then he returned to the palace, and, going to Yudhishṭhira, asked his leave to observe his vow by retiring to the woods. The young king, grieved and agitated, begged him to remain. "O hero, well do I know the reason why thou didst enter my chamber, and didst what thou regardest to be an act disagreeable to me. But there is no displeasure in my mind.........Desist from thy purpose. Do what I say. Thy virtue hath sustained no diminution. Thou hast not disregarded me." But Arjuna was not to be moved. "I have heard, even from thee, that quibbling is not permitted in the discharge of duty. I cannot waver from truth. Truth is my weapon."

This regard for truth is one of the most salient characteristics of the Áryans, and is continually coming out in this history. The love of truth, the horror of falsehood—these we find in men and women alike, in all castes and all ranks. An Áryan youth cannot tell a lie without shaming his ancestors.

So the blameless Arjuna set out on his exile, and

ere long, as he was bathing and performing his pûjâ, Ulupî, a water-nymph, the daughter of the king of the Nâgas, caught him round the waist and dragged him to the bottom of the stream into her palace. Interrupted in his worship in this unceremonious way, Arjuna, seeing a fire burning in the palace, quietly finished his devotions, and then asked the nymph why she had carried him off. She told him that she had fallen in love with him, and Arjuna yielded to her urgency and remained with her till the following morning. He then went on his way, meeting with many adventures, and visiting holy places, till he reached the land of Shrî Krishṇa, and the Holy One came to see His friend. Presently they went together to Dvârakâ, and there Arjuna saw the beautiful Subhadrâ, the sister of Shrî Krishṇa. He fell deeply in love with her, and Shrî Krishṇa advised him to carry her off by force, as this was a Kshattriya custom. Arjuna sent a message to Yudhishṭhira, and, receiving his consent, he watched his opportunity, and carried the maiden off in his chariot as she was walking with her attendants. These gave the alarm, and all the chiefs of the Yâdavas and Vrishnis gathered together, hot with anger, eager to pursue and fight with Arjuna. But Shrî Krishṇa soothed them with gentle words, praising Arjuna, and counselling them to go after him and bring him back in friendship, for where could be found for Subhadrâ a better husband than he? Then the chiefs did as He advised, and Arjuna lived in Dvârakâ for awhile, and, when the twelve years of exile were over, he returned to Indraprástha, accompanied by Keshava and Balarâma and many great warriors, and the Vrishnis brought as wedding gifts vast stores of wealth and animals. There, in Indraprastha, Subhadrâ gave birth to Abhimanyu, the favourite of Shri Krishṇa, whose life was to be so short and glorious; for he was Varchas, the son of the God Soma, who only allowed him to leave heaven for sixteen years, to fight on Kurukshetra, and from that field "my boy of mighty arms shall re-appear before me." [§ 201-223, 67.]

There to Keshava and Arjuna, sporting in the woods, came Agni one day in the guise of a Brâhmaṇa, asking their aid to consume the forest of Khâṇḍava, protected by Indra. Brahmâ had advised him to seek the help of Nara and Nârâyana, then on earth as Arjuna and Shrî Krishṇa, and he came to them begging for it. Arjuna said that he had no proper bow nor a sufficient supply of arrows, and he needed a car with swift horses, and a mighty weapon for Keshava. Then Agni thought of Varuṇa, the God of the waters, and, Varuṇa appearing in answer to his thought, Agni prayed him to give to Arjuna the great bow called Gâṇḍîva, and the inexhaustible quivers, and the ape-bannered car of king Soma, and to give to Shrî Krishṇa the discus of great fame. Varuṇa gave these weapons as he was asked, and Agni blazed forth in the forest of Khâṇḍava, and, when Indra sent clouds to pour down rain, Arjuna showered arrows on them and dispersed them. And for fifteen days the forest burned till it was destroyed, and only six living creatures escaped from it, one of whom was Maya, an Asura, who ran to Arjuna to protect him.

And when all was over, Indra, pleased with the skill and courage of his son, appeared to Keshava and Arjuna as they were resting, and offered them a boon. Then Arjuna asked Indra to give him his celestial weapons, and Indra answered: "When the illustrious Mahâdeva becomes pleased with thee, then, O son of Pâṇḍu, I will give thee all my weapons." And "Vâsudeva [Shrî Krishṇa] asked that His friendship with Arjuna might be eternal." [§ 224-236.]

[END OF THE ÁDI PARVA.]

CHAPTER IV.

THE GATHERING OF THE STORM-CLOUDS

We now begin the second volume of the "Mahâbhârata", the Sabhâ Pârva, taking its name from the three fateful assemblies, the record of which makes up its contents.

You remember that in the burning of the forest of Khândava, Maya, a Dânava, escaped. In gratitude for the saving of his life by Arjuna, he was eager to do something in return; Arjuna answered kindly and courteously, but refused his offer of service, and, on Maya pressing the offer, bade him do something for Shrî Krishṇa: Vâsudeva, on reflection, desired him, since he was the foremost of artists, to build a splendid palace for Yudhishṭhira, and Maya consented with delight, and, returning to the capital, measured out a large piece of land as site for the building. [§ 1.]

Shrî Krishṇa just then went away home, and we may delay a moment to mark the reverence He ever showed to His elders—He who was God. In taking farewell, He made obeisance with His head to the feet of His father's sister, and worshipped the Brâhmaṇas, Yudhishṭhira and Bhîma—the two latter being His seniors [§ 2.] On another occasion we read that He "was engaged at His own will in washing the feet of the Brâhmaṇas." [§ 35.] He did not shew the modern spirit of careless disrespect, but set the example of the most dutiful reverence to those who, physically, were His superiors.

Maya informed the Pâṇḍavas that he had once, during a sacrifice near lake Vindu by the Dânavas, gathered large stores of precious stones ; in the lake were also a club belonging to the king of the Dânavas and Varuṇa's great conch, Devadatta. He went thither and brought back all these treasures, giving the club to Bhîma, the conch-shell to Arjuna, and using the gems for the building of a wonderful palace. It had golden walls, and arches on golden columns, and flowers of gems floating on a tank with crystal steps and embankments of marble set with pearls. And round were blossoming trees of fragrant scents, and tanks with swans and other aquatic birds and lotuses. In fourteen months the peerless palace was ready, and a great opening ceremony was held to which came kings from many countries—the first Sabhâ, or assembly, recorded in this volume. [§ 3, 4.]

Hither came Nârada, a great Rishi, and "beholding the learned Rishi arrive, the eldest of the Pâṇḍavas, conversant with all rules of duty, quickly stood up with his younger brothers. Bending low with humility, the monarch cheerfully saluted the Rishi" with all proper forms, and then Nârada put questions to the king to see if he properly carried out his duties. The king, according to Hindu teaching, stands at the head of a nation, vested with Divine authority. He has the heaviest duties and the heaviest responsibilities, the most unceasing labour demanding the most incessant industry. If he be good, all goes well with his people, and he is answerable for the welfare and prosperity of the State. Later, we shall hear Bhîshma on the duties of a king; now, Nârada questions Yudhishṭhira. Does he divide his time judiciously, giving to religion, pleasure and profit severally its rightful share? Does he choose his ministers wisely and pay his troops regularly? Does he support the wives and children of the men who had given their lives for him in battle, and protect his conquered foes? Is he equally accessible to all, and "can every one approach thee without fear as if thou wast their mother and father?" Is his expenditure covered by a fourth, a third, or a half of his income? Are the agriculturists contented? "Are large tanks and lakes established all over thy kingdom at proper distances, without agriculture being in thy realm entirely dependent on the showers of heaven? The agriculturalists in thy kingdom want not either seed or food?" Does he make loans of seed to the tillers, and see that honest men manage agriculture, trade, cattle-rearing, and lending on interest? Does he ever commit injustice from covetousness, folly or pride? Are his ministers above bribery? Does he see that taxes are not unjustly levied? Does he give artisans wages and materials at intervals of not more than four months? Does he protect his kingdom from dangers, and "cherishest thou, like a father, the blind, the lame, the dumb, the deformed, the friendless and ascetics that have no homes? Hast thou banished these six evils, O monarch, sleep, idleness, fear, anger, weakness of mind, procrastination?" Then Yudhishṭhira bowed down to Nârada, worshipping his feet, and promising to fulfil the duties on which he had been questioned, and Nârada then described to the assembly some of the celestial palaces [§ 5-11.]

Now it appeared from his account that only one king, Harishchandra, was living in the palace of Indra, and Yudhishṭhira enquired as to his merits and also asked for news of his own father. Nârada answered that Harishchandra had performed the Râjasuya sacrifice, thus gaining the heaven of Indra, and that Pâṇḍu wished his son Yudhishṭhira to conquer the earth and perform the Râjasuya sacrifice, so that he, as his father, sharing his son's merit, might attain to the same place. This message Nârada brought to Yudhishthira, warning him, at the same time, of the difficulties attendant on the sacrifice. At it, the performer of the sacrifice was acclaimed as emperor, and the kings of the earth would only submit to a monarch at once righteous and powerful. Yudhishthira questioned himself and his counsellors as to whether he was worthy to perform this sacrifice. Now the state of his kingdom was the proof of his righteousness as king. He "was always kind to his subjects, working for the good of all, without making any distinctions." The people called him Ajâtashatru, "having no one as enemy." He "cherished every one as belonging to his family," and his brothers loyally aided him. "Owing to all this, the kingdom became free from disputes and fear of every kind. And all the people became attentive to their respective occupations. The rains became so abundant as to leave no room for desire; and the kingdom grew in prosperity.........Indeed, during the reign of Yudhishthira, who was ever devoted to truth, there was no extortion, no stringent realisation of arrears of rent, no fear of disease, of fire, or of death by poisoning and incantations in the kingdom." To this good and gentle king his counsellors with one voice said that he was worthy to perform the sacrifice. He, however, still revolved the matter in his mind, reckoning up his resources, not over-hasty, but remembering "that the wise never come to grief owing to their always acting after full deliberation." He finally decided to send to Shrî Krishṇa and ask for his advice, knowing that he could find no better counsellor.

Shrî Krishṇa quickly came at His friend's request, and, when He heard of the proposed sacrifice, He declared that one great obstacle stood in the way. Yudhishṭhira, indeed, was worthy to perform the sacrifice, but he could only offer it if he were acknowledged by all the kings as their chief, and there was one king, Jarâsandha of mighty power, who would never bow down to him as lord. Now Jarâsandha intended to offer a terrible human sacrifice, in which the victims were to be one hundred in number, each one a king. Eighty-six kings he had conquered and was then holding captive; thus only fourteen more were wanted to complete the tale. The man who prevented Jarâsandha from accomplishing this crime, said Shrî Krishṇa, "will surely win blazing renown." So he counselled attack on Jarâsandha. [§ 12-15].

It was decided, after some discussion, that it was useless to fight Jarâsandha with an army—his strength was too great. Better let Shrî Krishṇa go to him with Bhîma and Arjuna; in Him was policy, in Bhîma strength, in Arjuna prosperity. But Yudhishṭhira objected to the danger they would run, till: "if thou knowest my heart, if thou hast any faith in me," said Shrî Krishṇa finally, "then make over to me, as a pledge, Bhîma and Arjuna without loss of time." At this, Yudhishṭhira gave way, respectfully saying that he was under His command; let Arjuna "follow Krishṇa, the foremost of the Yâdavas, and let Bhîma follow Arjuna. Policy and good fortune and might will bring about success." Then the three heroes dressed themselves up as Snâtaka Brâhmaṇas and set out for Magadha, the capital of Jarâsandha. But unlike peaceful Brâhmaṇas, they broke down, as they approached Magadha, the peak of a mountain worshipped by the inhabitants, entered the city by an improper gate, and passing through the streets, violently seized garlands and robes wherewith to deck themselves. Arrived at the palace, they saw king Jarâsandha, who quickly rose up to receive them as Brâhmaṇas, but they would not accept his worship, Keshava asking him to see them after midnight. When the king came, he began to question his guests as to their strange behaviour. Snâtaka Brâhmaṇas did not deck themselves with flowers and sandal-paste, nor break down hills, nor come into a city with violence. Shrî Krishṇa answered gravely that Kshattriyas and Vaishyas could observe the Snâtaka vow as well as Brâhmaṇas, that flowers denoted prosperity, that "an enemy's abode should be entered through a wrong gate," and that "having entered the foe's abode for the accomplishment of our purpose, we accept not the worship offered to us." Surprised, king Jarâsandha demanded to know his offence, and Shrî Krishṇa told him that it lay in his proposal to offer human beings in sacrifice to Rudra. This crime they were there to prevent. And declaring His name and those of His companions, he concluded: "O king of Magadha, we challenge thee! Fight standing before us! Either set free all the monarchs, or go thou to the abode of Yama" (the king of death). King Jarâsandha accepted the challenge, and, installing his son on the throne, he chose Bhîma as his lopponent. For fourteen days they wrestled, and at last Bhîma, feeling his foe yielding, caught him in his terrible grip, whirled him round, and broke his back against his knee. Then Shrî Krishṇa set free the kings, and, mounting on Jarâsandha's famous celestial car, drove away with the brothers from the scene of victory. The liberated kings and Jarâsandha's son all accepted Yudhishṭhira as lord paramount, and the warriors returned home in triumph. [§ 16-24.]

The four younger brothers then set out with armies, Arjuna to the north, Bhîma to the east, Sahadeva to the south, and Nakula to the west—laying all nations under tribute to Yudhishṭhira. Here lay the strength of the Pâṇḍavas. All done by the four brothers was done for their elder brother. All they conquered, they conquered for him. All they gained, they gained for him. Each returning, laden with wealth, they "presented all that wealth to Yudhishṭhira." Thus the great sacrifice became possible. [§ 25-33.]

In reading the "Mahâbhârata", one is continually reminded of the wealth of India in ancient days, in the days when she put religion first and worldly matters second. As she sank down from her spiritual pre-eminence, she became weak, she fell a prey to conquerors, and her vast treasures were gradually dispersed. We find gorgeous buildings with well-built walls, windows covered with network of gold, interiors decorated with rows of pearls, staircases strewn with costly carpets. [§ 34.] We find among the tribute brought to king Yudhishṭhira not only vast stores of gems and golden coins, but golden jars and plate, ivory-handled and gem-decked swords, inlaid armour, cars splendidly adorned, fine blankets of wool, clothes woven from jute and from the threads of insects, rich carpets, costly beds, gold-embroidered stuffs, silks, perfumes, sandalwood. Thousands of elephants, horses, mules, asses, are sent, decked with splendid housings. Everywhere there is evidence of artistic taste, as well as of the most gorgeous magnificence. Nothing could shew more plainly the high civilisation of ancient India, her uncounted wealth, her abundant prosperity, than the descriptions of great ceremonies given in such books as the "Mahâbhârata" and the "Râmâyana," books of unchallenged antiquity. In addition to this, there is evidence of widely spread abundance and prosperity among the masses of the people; we see shops running over with goods, citizens' houses gaily decked for pageants. Where the blessings of the Gods are gained by piety, reverence, dutifulness and charity, there all good things are found, material wealth among them.

To the sacrifice came kings from all quarters, and Nakula was sent to Hastinâpura to formally invite Bhîshma and Dhritarâshṭra. Thither came also Vidura and Droṇa and the sons of Dhritarâshṭra, with Karṇa and Kripa, and all the heroes who play great parts in our story. Yudhishṭhira placed the whole treasure at the command of Bhîshma and Droṇa and his elders, begging them to direct everything. All went well till the last day, when Yudhishṭhira was to be sprinkled with sacred water as emperor. As Nârada looked round on the vast assembly of kings—the second great Sabhâ of this volume—he remembered what he had heard of the deities taking birth as men, and of Nârâyana Himself becoming incarnate, and, thinking that He would ere long sweep away the vast concourse, he sat there filled with awe. The first war cry of the coming struggle was, indeed, there uttered. For Bhîshma called for the offering of Arghyas to the kings, each in his turn and first to the foremost. Asked Yudhishṭhira: "Whom dost thou deem the foremost among these?" and Bhîshma answered, indicating Shrî Krishṇa: "As the sun among all luminous objects, so doth this one shine like the sun among all these." Then Sahadeva offered the first Arghya to Keshava, who duly accepted it. At that up sprang Sishupâla, king of Chedi, hotly reproaching the Pâṇḍavas and Bhîshma as ignorant of duty; this Krishṇa was not even a king, nor was he the eldest, nor the guru, nor the priest; in every aspect, there was a man higher than he; why were the monarchs brought there to be insulted by the offer of worship to one who was no king? And Sishupâla turned to leave the assembly in anger, followed by the kings. Then Yudhishṭhira ran after him, softly entreating him, but Bhîshma said sternly: "He that approveth not the worship offered unto Krishṇa, the Oldest One in the universe, deserveth neither soft words nor consideration." And, in words weighty and wise, he extolled the Holy One, there present in human form. Then Sahadeva challenged any who resented the worship offered to Shrî Krishṇa, Father and Guru, and Nakula said: "Those men that will not worship Krishṇa, with eyes like lotus leaves, should be regarded as dead though moving, and should never be talked to on any occasion."

Then the great assembly became agitated, and to Yudhishṭhira, anxious that his sacrifice should not be obstructed, Bhîshma spoke calmly, telling him that the dog could not slay the lion, and that Achyuta (Shrî Krishṇa) was "like a lion that is asleep." Sishupâla broke out again in passionate reproaches, until Bhîma leapt up to attack him, but was restrained by Bhîshma, who recounted the story of Sishupâla, saying that he was destined to be slain by Shrî Krishṇa, who had promised his mother to pardon him for one hundred offences. The war of words raged hotly, till Bhîshma declared that they had worshipped Govinda, and abode by their act; let him who wished for speedy death challenge the wielder of the discus and the macc—for he knew that the time had come for Sishupâla to be slain by Shrî Krishṇa. Then Sishupâla challenged Shrî Krishṇa, who answered softly, recounting his former offences, pardoned for his mother's sake, till now the hundred were fulfilled. And as Sishupâla again spoke angrily, the Lord thought of His discus and it came to His hand, and, rushing at His foe, struck off his head, so that he fell "like a cliff struck by lightning." With his fall came peace. Shrî Krishṇa Himself guarded the conclusion of the sacrifice, and Yudhishṭhira was raised to the imperial dignity, acclaimed by all the kings. Then the kings departed to their own countries, and Shrî Krishṇa to Dvârakâ; but, ere leaving, Vyâsa told Yudhishṭhira of the evil times to come and of the destruction of the Kshattriyas in a quarrel for his sake. So Yudhishṭhira, crowned emperor and prosperous, was left sad at heart, and vowed to speak no harsh word lest he should cause disagreement that might bring on war. [§ 34-46.]

For awhile Duryodhana remained behind with the Pâṇḍavas, and, accompanied by Shakuni, examined the splendid palace built by Maya. And he was several times deceived by Maya's cunning devices.

He drew up his robe on crossing a crystal surface, fancying it was water, and then fell into a lake, believing it to be crystal. He struck his head against a crystal door, seeing nothing in his way, and, guarding himself against this blunder, fell through an open door, thinking it closed. And Bhîma laughed aloud at his blunders, as did Arjuna and the twins, and even the servants, and Duryodhana was angry, and at last went away home with envy and wrath in his heart. Bitterly he complained to his uncle Shakuni, king of Gândhâra, and threatened to kill himself. "Beholding their sovereignty over the world, their vast wealth and also that sacrifice, who is there like me that would not smart under all that?" "The sons of Dhritarâshṭra are decaying and the sons of Prithâ are growing day by day." Shakuni sought to comfort him, pointing out how great were his own resources; if this did not satisfy him, then, while the Pâṇḍavas could not be vanquished by force—they were too strong—none the less they might be overcome by guile. Then he spoke the fateful words: "The son of Kuntî is very fond of gambling, although he doth not know how to play. That king, if asked to play, is ill able to refuse. I am skilful at dice. There is none equal to me on earth, no, not even in the three worlds, O son of Kuru! Therefore ask him to play at dice. Skilled at dice, I will win his kingdom and that splendid prosperity of his for thee, O bull among men. But, O Duryodhana, represent all this unto the king. Commanded by thy father, I will win without doubt the whole of Yudhishṭhira's possessions." Thus spoke the crafty Shakuni, moved by love for his nephew. To Dhritarâshṭra he went and told him of Duryodhana's grief, and the blind king, sending for his eldest son, gently chid him for his folly. But headstrong Duryodhana, in answer, only poured out his envious feelings bitterly, and Shakuni proposed to play at dice with Yudhishṭhira for his possessions. Dhritarâshṭra refused to consent without consulting Vidura, and sent for his younger brother, despite Duryodhana's cry that if his father did not yield he would kill himself, and "when I am dead, O king, thou wilt become happy with Vidura." When Vidura came, Dhritarâshṭra told him that he had decided to let the challenge go, and would send him as messenger to bring Yudhishṭhira; but while Vidura went to Bhîshma in great sorrow, the blind king sent again for his eldest son, and begged him to give up his purpose. Duryodhana, however, stood obstinately against his father's entreaties, describing again, with much detail, the wealth and glory of the Pâṇḍavas, and bitterly recalling the blunders he had made in their wondrous palace. Dhritarâshṭra pleaded to him to cease from his envy: "O son, be not jealous of the Pâṇḍavas. He that is jealous is always unhappy, and suffereth the pangs of death......O child, coveting others' possessions is exceedingly weak. He, on the other hand enjoyeth happiness who is content with his own." Still Duryodhana pressed for his way and urged the match at dice, until his father yielded unwillingly, foreboding the evil that was coming. "The weak-minded Dhritarâshṭra regarded fate as supreme and unavoidable," forgetting that man creates his own destiny and that as long as he is able to think, he is able to change. Vidura uttered a last protest: "I approve not, O king, of this command of thine. Do not act so. I fear this will bring about the destruction of our race." None the less being "commanded against his will" by his elder brother and sovereign, Vidura set out for Khândavaprastha to carry the fateful challenge.

Arrived there, he delivered the king's message, inviting Yudhishṭhira to repair to the newly erected palace of his uncle and to "sit for a friendly match at dice." At once Yudhishṭhira objected that the match might lead to a quarrel; what did Vidura advise? Vidura answered that "gambling is the root of misery, and I strove to dissuade the king from it. The king however, hath sent me to thee." Yudhishṭhira must do what was best. "O learned one," said the king, "I do not desire, at the command of Dhritarâshṭra, to engage in gambling." But there came in the duty of the Kshattriya, never to refuse a challenge. "Unwilling as I am to gamble, I will not do so if the wicked Shakuni doth not summon me to it in the Sabhâ. If, however, he challengeth me, I will never refuse. For that, as settled, is my eternal vow."

Sadly the young king set forth, with his brothers and his wife, on the fatal journey. Deep hidden in his nature was the love of gambling, though firmly held in check by his self-control. The Gods so guided events as to burn it out of his nature, and to give an object-lesson for all time as to the mischief wrought by this vice. Arrived at Hastinâpura, they were royally lodged in the new palace, and the third great Sabhâ, that which witnessed the ruin of the Pâṇḍavas, was complete. [§ 47-58.]

Shakuni, the wily gamester, challenged the young king, who made one last protest in favour of, at least, fair play. But Shakuni audaciously declared that he hoped to win, and mockingly bade Yudhishṭhira, "If thou art under any fear, then desist from play." Stung by the taunt, Yudhishṭhira proudly answered:

"Summoned, I do not withdraw. This is my established vow." But who could stake against him on equal terms? Duryodhana staked his wealth, naming his uncle Shakuni as his representative in throwing the dice. Yudhishṭhira uttered a hopeless objection: "Gambling for oneself by the agency of another seemeth to me to be contrary to rule. Thou also, O learned one, wilt admit this. If, however, thou art still bent on it, let the play begin."

The great match opened, the king staking a wreath of pearls set in gold; Shakuni threw and cried: "Lo, I have won!" Then the king staked his wealth of gold, silver, minerals, and again "Lo, I have won!" said Shakuni. His royal car was Yudhishṭhira's next stake; using unfair means, Shakuni called: "Lo, I have won." Then the king set his female slaves, and again came the answer, "Lo, I have won!" His male slaves; "Lo, I have won!" Elephants, well trained in war, with their mates. Still the monotonous refrain: "Lo, I have won!" Battle cars with trained horses and warriors. "Lo, I have won!" Steeds of purest, even of celestial, breeds. "Lo, I have won!" Vehicles and draught animals and picked warriors. "Lo, I have won!" Jewels of fabulous value. "Lo, I have won!" Then Vidura broke in, unable to bear the growing ruin, and prayed Dhritarâshṭra to intervene. "Gambling is the root of dissensions. It bringeth about disunion. Its consequences are frightful.........Duryodhana is gambling with the son of Pâṇḍu, and thou art in raptures that he is winning. It is such success that begetteth war, which endeth in the destruction of men.........What dost thou gain by winning from the Pâṇḍavas their vast wealth? Win the Pâṇḍavas themselves, who will be more to thee than all the wealth they have. We all know the skill of Suvala [Shakuni] in play. This hill king knoweth many nefarious methods in gambling. Let Shakuni return whence he came. War not, O Bhârata, with the sons of Pâṇḍu!" Duryodhana answered angrily, taunting Vidura with his partiality for the Pâṇḍavas though he was the servant of the Kurus. With bitter words he bade his uncle leave them and go whither he would. "A wife that is unchaste, however well-treated, forsaketh her husband yet." Deeply wounded, Vidura turned to the blind king, asking his impartial judgment. He then told the angry prince that if he would always hear pleasant words, no matter what his conduct, he must seek the weak for his friends. "A sinful man speaking words that are agreeable may be had in this world. But a speaker of words that are disagreeable, though fit as regimen, or a hearer of the same, is very rare. He indeed is a king's true ally, who, disregarding what is agreeable or disagreeable to his master, beareth himself virtuously and uttereth what may be disagreeable but required as regimen. O great king, drink thou that which the honest drink and the dishonest shun, even humility, which is like a medicine that is bitter, pungent, burning, unintoxicating, disagreeable and revolting. And, drinking it, O king, regain thou thy sobriety." Then Vidura bowed as in leave-taking, sad at heart.

The game goes on. Yudhishṭhira stakes all his remaining wealth in coin, untold in value. Again the cry arises, "Lo, I have won!" He pledges all his cattle, horses, sheep and goats. "Lo, I have won!" His city and land, the wealth of all his subjects, save that of Brâhmaṇas. "Lo, I have won!" His subject kings. "Lo, I have won!" Stripped of all his possessions, of his servants, his subjects, his princes, surely Yudhishṭhira is now utterly despoiled. What else remains? Alas! the fever of the gambler is upon him. The band of brothers is still unbroken. He is not yet wholly without wealth. What are these wild words that break from his white lips? "This Nakula here, of mighty arms and leonine neck, of red eyes, and endued with youth, is now my one stake. Know that he is my wealth." There is a ring of triumph in the reply: "Lo, he hath been won by us!" The peerless circle of brothers is broken. The end comes swiftly on, and quickly Sahadeva is staked. And again shrills out the cry, "Lo, I have won!" Arjuna next, the ever-victorious, "the one bow in this world," with him as stake "I will now play with thee." "Lo, I have won!" Bhîma, the mightiest, remains, and he is staked and lost. "Lo, I have won!" "Say," cries Shakuni mockingly, "if thou hast anything which thou hast not lost?" The maddened king stakes himself, and again the cry rings out: "Lo, I have won!" The royal brothers are now not only paupers; they are—last shame of all for the Kshattriya—slaves, slaves in the hands of their foes. Surely their ruin is complete, their fall beyond remedy. What other blow remains for fate to strike?

The smooth voice of Shakuni breaks the silence. "O king, there is yet one stake dear to thee that is still unwon. Stake thou Krishṇâ, the princess of Panchâla. By her, win thyself back." Surely, at this last insult, the proud young king will awaken from his fatal madness, the madness of the gambler. What thoughts sweep over him, as her sweet name falls from the lips of his despoiler! Krishnâ, whose maiden loveliness had won his heart. Krishnâ, whose loving faithfulness had served him loyally. Krishnâ, who had guided so wisely his royal household. Krishnâ, who had lain in his bosom, who was the mother of his son. Would he stake her, his wife, the glory and honour of his race? Listen, as her praises fall from his quivering lips; yet still the gambler triumphs, mixed with who can say what of Kshattriya and king, grimly resolute to fight to the last gasp? He puts Draupadî on the throw of the fatal dice: "making the slender-waisted Draupadî my stake, I will play with thee, O son of Suvala!" Cries of "Fie! Fie!" arise as the young king thus stakes his wife: the whole assembly is agitated, men weep or laugh as their sympathies run, great kings are sobbing; over the tumult rises for the last time the exultant cry: "Lo, I have won!" All is over; the play is played; everything is lost.

Then cried Duryodhana, mocking, to Vidura to go and fetch the dearly-loved wife of the Pâṇḍavas. "Let her sweep the chambers," he shouted, let her "stay where our serving-women are." Vidura answered sadly, warningly, but Duryodhana was not to be stayed in the headlong rush of his triumph. He bade a servant go and fetch Draupadî, and the man, "entering the abode of the Pâṇḍavas, like a dog a lion's den, approached the queen of the sons of Pâṇḍu," and told her roughly that Duryodhana had won her at dice, and that he would put her to some menial work. The queen, surprised, asked what had happened, and on learning that Yudhishṭhira had staked his brothers, then himself, and lastly her, she saw, with her quick woman's wit, a way of escape. Go and ask, she said, "whom he hath lost first, himself or me." Returning, the messenger repeated her words, but Yudhishṭhira, stricken with grief, gave no answer. Then Duryodhana bade bring her to the assembly and let her say there what she would, and the messenger, shamed at heart at the outrage, went back and deprecatingly executed his mission. Draupadî sent him back to ask the elders what she should do, professing her willingness to obey them, and the messenger again went back and repeated her words. Yudhishṭhira now, remembering that he had lost her, crushing down his outraged honour, sent to bid her come. As Duryodhana's messenger hesitated, fearing to commit the outrage of bringing her there, the headstrong prince bade his younger brother, Dushâsana, go and bring Krishṇâ thither by force. Forth went Dushâsana on his shameful errand, and mockingly bade the gentle lady put aside her modesty and face the great assembly. Then Draupadî, in despair, leapt up and fled towards the dwelling of the ladies of the royal household, but Dushâsana rushed after her and, catching her by her long streaming locks, he dragged her with cruel force into the Sabhâ. Alas for her, the cherished wife, on whom no rough wind had blown, no unfriendly eye had rested, dragged by her hair—so lately sanctified by the waters of consecration—into a riotous assembly, exposed there to the rude gaze of men, half-naked, a single cloth wrapped round her shrinking body. Maddened by outraged modesty, her anger rose and Krishṇâ cried to the learned, nay, to the very warriors, to stop, for even shame's sake, an act so unworthy of their order. Were all afraid? "Why do those foremost of the Kuru elders look silently on this great crime?"

There sat her husbands, her lords—was there no help in them? Alas, they were bound by their duty, and might not rescue her, and Dushâsana, knowing their helplessness, shook her yet more roughly, crying, "Slave! Slave!" and Karṇa laughed aloud, and Shakuni, but these, with Dushâsana and Duryodhana, were all that rejoiced in sweet Krishṇâ's shame. Then Bhîshma spake slowly and sadly; he could not decide the point raised; Yudhishṭhira having lost himself had nought to stake, yet was a wife ever under the command of her lord. "I cannot decide," he said. Where Bhîshma hesitated, who should be sure, and solution there seemed none. Dushâsana continued his rough usage, till the piteous plight of his loved one at last moved Bhîma beyond all endurance, and he broke forth in wrath. Bitterly he reproached Yudhishṭhira for staking her; all else might have gone, but not the wife. "For her sake, O king, my anger falleth on thee. I shall burn those hands of thine. Sahadeva, bring fire!" The lion's roar rolled round the dumb assembly, but Arjuna, the blameless, spake rebukingly, holding himself in strong control: Yudhishṭhira had upheld the Kshattriya usage, playing against his will at the challenge of the foe; besides, who might speak against the eldest brother? Then Bhîma answered, mastering his rage by a mighty effort: "If I had not known, O Dhananjaya [Arjuna], that the king had acted according to Kshattriya usage, then, taking his hands together by sheer force, I would have burned them in a blazing fire."

At last Vikarṇa, a younger brother of Duryodhana, spoke, urgently appealing to the assembled kings to decide the question raised by Krishṇâ. Failing to obtain an answer, he boldly declared that for his part, he regarded Draupadî as not won. The kings loudly applauded this declaration, but Karṇa sharply reproved Vikarṇa for thus speaking before his elders and superiors. And he went on to justify the treatment of Krishṇâ, and bade Dushâsana take off the robes of the Pâṇḍavas and strip Draupadî. Then the Pâṇḍavas flung off their upper garments, and Dushâsana began to drag off the sole covering worn by Krishṇâ. Bereft of ḥuman protection, shut out from help of man, the daughter of the sacrificial fire cried aloud in her agony to Him who ever befriends the helpless. "O Govinda! O Thou that dwellest in Dvârakâ! O Krishṇa!" and so, with many another name, she called. And Shrî Krishṇa, hearing, was deeply moved and came. And Dharma, standing by unseen, covered Krishṇâ with clothes of many hues. And as one robe was dragged off another was seen, and so on till hundreds were heaped upon the floor, and Dushâsana, tired and ashamed, sat down. Again rang out the lion's roar of Bhîma, and dread was the oath he swore. "Hear these words of mine, ye Kshattriyas of the world. Words such as these were never before uttered by other men, nor will be uttered in the future. Ye lords of earth, if, having spoken these words, I do not accomplish them hereafter, let me not obtain the path of my deceased ancestors! Tearing open in battle, by sheer force, the breast of this wretch, this wicked-minded scoundrel of the Bhâratas—if I do not drink his life-blood, let me not obtain the path of my ancestors!" Terrible pledge, to be terribly redeemed.

Still was the weeping Krishṇâ left without an answer, and Karṇa bade Dushâsana, "Take away this serving-woman Krishṇâ to the inner apartments." Again he began to drag at her, she looking appealingly round. Then said Duryodhana craftily that she should appeal to her husbands. Let them declare "Yudhishṭhira not to be their lord, let them make king Yudhishṭhira the just a liar, then shalt thou be freed from slavery. Let the illustrious son of Dharma, always adhering to virtue, who is even like Indra himself, declare whether he is, or is not, thy lord! "Then Bhîma cried, waving his mighty arms, that king Yudishṭhira the just was truly their lord. He is the lord of all our religious and ascetic merits, the lord of even our lives! If he regardeth himself as won, we too have all been won." Karṇa mockingly bade Krishṇâ go to her service, and choose another husband, "one who will not make thee a slave by gambling." "Obedient to the king and bound by the tie of virtue and duty," Bhîma sat breathing hard, "a very picture of woe." Duryodhana challenged Yudhishṭhira to answer, and then, to exasperate Bhîma, insultingly uncovered his left thigh in the sight of Draupadî. Furiously Bhîma shouted: "Let not Vrikodara [Bhîma] attain to the regions obtained by his ancestors, if he doth not break that thigh of thine in the great conflict." The second awful pledge given by Bhîma to the future.

At last, appeal was made to the blind king, and he, desirous of warding off destruction, spoke softly to Krishṇâ, and bade her ask of him any boon she would. At once she asked for the freedom of Yudhishṭhira, that her son might not be called the son of a slave. Granting this, the king bade her choose a second boon, and she chose the liberty of the four brothers with their weapons. This was granted, and a third boon proffered. This Krishṇâ refused, declaring that her husbands, set free, could themselves achieve prosperity. Truly did Karṇa say that Draupadî, "becoming as a boat to the sons of Pâṇḍu, who were sinking in a boatless ocean of distress, hath brought them in safety to the shore."

Then Yudhishṭhira, having calmed Bhîma, approached Dhritarâshṭra with joined hands, and prayed him to give his orders, for they desired to remain in obedience to him. The blind king bade him return home and rule his kingdom, urging him to follow counsels of peace, to forget the harshness of Duryodhana and remember only Gândhârî and himself. But, as the brothers were setting forth, Duryodhana went in haste to the king, and, pointing out that the

Pâṇḍavas were infuriated, urged on him the danger of letting them go. He begged that one more throw of the dice might take place, the losers to go to the woods for twelve years, and then remain for one year, unrecognised, in some inhabited country; if they were recognised, another twelve years' exile should follow. Despite the pleading of Droṇa, Vidura, Bhîshma and other leading men, the king consented, aye, though even Gândhârî begged him to abandon Duryodhana. The Pândavas were recalled and the stake declared, with the addition that on the expiry of the thirteenth year the kingdom of the exiled was to be restored to them. Yudhishṭhira sadly sat down once more, to play for this last stake, and for the last time the cry of Shakuni was heard: "Lo, I have won!"

Then the sons of Pâṇḍu cast off their royal robes and clad themselves in deer skins, Dushâsana loudly exulting over them and bidding Krishṇâ forsake them and choose another lord. And Bhîma, "like a Himâlayan lion," approached him, rebuking him, but "without doing anything, for he could not deviate from the path of virtue," and Dushâsana shouted at him, dancing the while, "O cow! O cow!" Bhîma, suppressing his rage, followed his eldest brother, prophesying sternly the slaughter that should come. But

G

Arjuna said softly: "O Bhîma, the resolutions of high-minded men are not known in words only. On the fourteenth year from this day, they shall see what happeneth." There spake the strong man, speaking by deeds. Each of the four younger brothers formally registered a solemn vow to slay their enemies and then went to bid respectful farewell to king Dhritarâshṭra. When Yudhishṭhira spoke his brief and sad farewell, none was able to answer him for very shame, but "within their hearts, however, they prayed" for his welfare. Then Vidura bade them leave their mother in his charge, and declared to them that they would reap great benefit from their exile; they would gain in it, rightly used, forces that no foe would be able to withstand. "O son of Kuntî, with our leave go hence. O Bhârata, blessings be thine. No one can say that ye have done anything sinful. We hope to see thee, therefore, return in safety and crowned with success." Sad was the parting between the heart-broken Kuntî and her sons; scarce could she master her woe and tear herself away. At last, all was over, and the mournful procession filed forth. Yudhishṭhira went first, covering his face; Bhîma, looking at his strong arms; Arjuna, scattering sand; Sahadeva, besmearing his face; Nakula, staining himself with dust; Krishṇâ, weeping and covering her face with her dishevelled hair; Dhaumya, with kusha grass in hand, uttering "the awful mantras of the Samaveda, relating to Yama."

Dhritarâshṭra anxiously enquired of Vidura, who brought him the news of the going forth, what was the meaning of the actions of the Pânḍavas. And Vidura said that king Yudhishṭhira, ever kind, would not let his eyes light on any lest they should be injured by his wrath; that Bhîma was longing for the day when his strong arms should wreak his vengeance on his foes; that Arjuna scattered sand as emblem of the arrows he would scatter in battle; that Sahadeva would avoid recognition in the day of trouble; that Nakula stained his face with dust that he might win no heart by love; that Draupadî thought of the wives of her enemies, who in fourteen years would be bewailing their husbands on that very road; and that Dhaumya was chanting beforehand the obsequies that would accompany the dead.

Then nature bewailed the crime that had been wrought and the coming woes, and Nârada, surrounded by great Rishis, appeared and said: "On the fourteenth year hence, the Kauravas, in consequence of Duryodhana's fault, will all be destroyed by the might of Bhîma and Arjuna." On which they vanished, as suddenly as they came. Thus in gloom and fateful presage set the sun that witnessed the exile of the Pâṇḍavas.

—:o:—

CHAPTER V.

THE THIRTEEN YEARS' EXILE.

We have now to follow the Pâṇḍavas and their wife through their twelve years of wanderings in woods and on mountains and their year of disguise in a city—thirteen years of trial and anxiety. This part of our story is told in two Parvas; the twelve years in the jungles are described in the Vana (wood) Parva, and the story of the year in disguise is told in the Virâta Parva—Virâta being the name of the king of the city where it was spent.

The first of these, the Vana Parva, is very bulky: it is the longest of all the Parvas except one, the Shânti Parva. This is due to the fact that it contains some very long and instructive discourses, delivered to the princes by Rishis who visited them, and also some beautiful stories told to amuse, as well as to teach them, in the weary days of exile. We shall have to leave these out, but you might read them for yourselves as you have time. You will find in this Parva part of the story of Râma, the Avatâra, the divine King; and the story of Sâvitrî who, by her devotion and cleverness won back her husband from the arms of death—a lovely story; and the tale of king Nala and his wife Damayantî, and of all the sorrows they underwent in consequence of Nala's gambling. The princes learned a great deal during their exile, as you may also learn, if you follow their footsteps through the Vana Parva.

When the princes set out from Hastinâpura they were followed by a great crowd of people, who wished to go with them, instead of remaining under the rule of Duryodhana; they declared that they wished to associate with the good, not with the bad, for association with the righteous brought religious merit while association with the evil caused virtue to lessen. "We wish to live with you," they cried, "who possess those attributes" of goodness. The people were here stating a very important rule of conduct. We should try and live with those who are leading a good life, and should not go into bad company. One person affects another. You may catch smallpox by going among people suffering from that disease, and moral diseases are more catching and more serious than physical ones. The minds of good people send out purity, and the minds of bad people impurity. Both are catching. In choosing your companions, choose the good, especially while you are young; as you grow older, your characters will become more fixed, and you will be less liable to catch other people's habits than while you are young.

But Yudhishṭhira knew that the people had no right to leave their own king in order to follow him. So he begged them to go back, and to love and serve Bhîshma, Dhritarâshṭra, Vidura and Kuntî, and thus shew their love to himself and his brothers. If we have a bad ruler, we do not improve him by desertion or rebellion. We have the ruler we deserve, that our karma brings to us. If he be bad, we should make the best of him, and by doing our part of duty well, as loyal subjects, should steady the disturbed State. If we are rebellious, we are left to our own remedy and it goes ill with ruler and people alike; if we continue faithful and dutiful, the Gods see to our protection, as in this case, where Duryodhana was removed at the proper time by a righteous war, led by those whose duty it was to wage it. This is the old Hindu teaching, and it worked out much better for every body concerned than the modern way of agitation and rebellion. So the people went home at Yudhishṭhira's bidding, and the princes passed onwards to the banks of Gangâ, accompanied only by some Brâhmaṇas who surrounded them with holy chants.

On the following morning, Yudhishṭhira was much distressed because he had no food to give to the Brâhmaṇas, he who had ever fed them daily by thousands, and he prayed them to leave him, so that they should not suffer privation. They still clung to him, till he sank weeping on the ground, lamenting his inability to protect them. In vain one of them, named Saunaka, reminded him that he should not grieve over the loss of wealth, and bade him emancipate himself from desire for worldly possessions. He answered piteously that he did not desire wealth for himself, but only for the support of the Brâhmaṇas dependent on him; how could he neglect the duty of the householder? In eloquent words he praised the "eternal morality" of hospitality. "To the weary a bed, to one fatigued with standing a seat, to the thirsty water, and to the hungry food should ever be given. To the guest are due pleasant looks and a cheerful heart and sweet words." Then he turned to his priest and asked what he should do, and Dhaumya bade him pray to Sûrya Deva, the sun, and practise austerity and meditation; so should a way of escape be found. And the king, standing in Gangâ and practising prâṇâyâma (control of the breath), lifted up his heart to God as revealed in the Sun and praised him as the giver of all; and the

God appeared, blazing like fire, self-luminous, and blessed his worshipper, and gave him a copper bowl which should never be empty of food so long as Krishṇâ held it without partaking of its contents. Then Sûrya vanished, and Yudhishṭhira cooked a little food and placed it in the bowl held by his wife, and with that food, which became inexhaustible, he fed the Brâhmaṇas, and his brothers, and lastly himself. And when all had eaten, Krishṇâ took her meal, and then the bowl was empty. All through their wanderings they and theirs fed from this solar bowl, and knew no want. For all food comes from the light and heat of the Sun, and his action on earth and atmosphere, passing through many stages from the seed-corn to the full ear reaped in the harvest; and he can hasten the working if he will, and sometimes does so hasten it, when a faithful servant of His needs food for the helping of others, for unselfish charity.

Then began the regular life in the forest with all its privations and hardships. The princes were soon visited there by Vidura, who told them that Dhritarâshṭra had angrily dismissed him, because he begged him to discard Duryodhana and to call back the Pâṇḍavas. He advised Yudhishṭhira to be patient, telling him that the wise man, who could patiently endure gross wrong, ended by reaping success, and Yudhishṭhira promised to abide by his advice. But Dhritarâshṭra soon repented of his hasty action and called Vidura back, and Vidura, ever dutiful, returned and spoke lovingly to his elder brother, assuring him that his sons were dear to him as the Pâṇḍavas, only "as the latter are now in distress, my heart yearneth after them." Meanwhile Karṇa incited Duryodhana to pursue the Pâṇḍavas into the forest, and the Kuru princes "rushed out in a body to slay the sons of Pâṇḍu." But the great Vyâsa, "knowing by his inner vision" that they had set out with this evil intent appeared before them and sent them back, and then went to king Dhritarâshṭra, desiring him to restrain Duryodhana from mischief, else only ruin could befall. "O king of the earth, if thou desirest all the Kauravas to live, let thy son Duryodhana make peace with the Pâṇḍavas." As Vyâsa left, another great sage, Maitreya, came, and he remonstrated with the king for allowing such wrongs as had been perpetrated; on account of these, he said, "which are even like the acts of wretched outcastes, thou art not well thought of among the ascetics." Then Maitreya turned to Duryodhana and spoke very gently to him, begging him to be at peace with his cousins, but Duryodhana rudely slapped his own thigh and smiled mockingly at the great ascetic. Maitreya, at this, pronounced his fateful curse, that Duryodhana should reap the fruit of his insolence, and "in the great war which shall spring out of the wrongs perpetrated by thee, the mighty Bhîma shall break that thigh of thine with a stroke of his mace." Dhritarâshṭra tried to persuade the sage to recall his words, but he told him that his sentence could only be made void by Duryodhana making peace with the Pâṇḍavas; refusing to talk any longer, since his counsels were disregarded, the gentle Maitreya went his way, one of the many holy ones who sought to turn Duryodhana from his evil path and failed.

At this time Shrî Krishṇa went to the Pâṇḍavas to tell them why He had not appeared at the court of Dhritarâshṭra in time to stop the game at dice, and to Him Krishṇâ made a most piteous appeal, declaring that "husbands or sons, or friends or brothers, or father have I none! Nor have I thee, O thou slayer of Madhu, for ye all, beholding me treated so cruelly, sit still unmoved." The Lord consoled her, and promised her that she should again reign as queen over kings. "The heavens might fall, or the Himavat might split, the earth might be rent, or the waters of the ocean might dry up, but My words shall never be in vain." Yet Draupadî could not resign herself to patience, and we find her soon urging Yudhishṭhira to action, imploring him not to forgive the wrongs they had suffered. This drew from the young king an admirable discourse on forgiveness: "If the man who hath ill speeches from another returneth those speeches afterwards; if the injured man returneth his injuries; if the chastised person chastiseth in return; if fathers slay sons, and sons fathers; if husbands slay wives, and wives husbands; then, O Krishṇâ, how can birth take place in a world where anger thus prevails? One should forgive, under every injury...... He, indeed, is a wise and excellent person who hath conquered his wrath, and who sheweth forgiveness even when insulted, oppressed, and angered by a strong person. Forgiveness is Brahman; forgiveness is truth: forgiveness is stored ascetic merit; forgiveness protecteth the ascetic merit of the future; forgiveness is asceticism; forgiveness is holiness; and by forgiveness it is that the universe is held together. The man of wisdom should ever forgive, for when he is capable of forgiving every thing, he attaineth to Brahman." But Draupadî still answered angrily, and, assailing the order of the world, she bitterly declared that God played with His creatures according to His pleasure, like a child makes or destroys an earthen toy. What was the use of virtue, if the virtuous were plunged in suffering while the wicked were prosperous? Gently but firmly Yudhishṭhira answered her, praising her excellent phrases and well-chosen words, but "thou speakest, however, the language of atheism. O princess, I never act solicitous of the fruits of my actions. I give away, because it is my duty to give; I sacrifice, because it is my duty to sacrifice; I act virtuously, not from the desire of reaping the fruits of virtue, but of not transgressing the ordinances of the Vedas, and beholding also the conduct of the good and wise. My heart, O Krishṇâ, is naturally attracted towards virtue. The man who wishes to reap the fruits of virtue is a trader in virtue. His nature is mean, and he should never be counted among the virtuous." None the less was it true, he went on, that acts had fruits, and that in the long run, under the providence of God, the practice of virtue was the source of prosperity. But the details of providence could only be understood by the wise, by those in whose minds dwelt quiet and peace and holiness. "Therefore, though thou mayst not see the fruits of virtue, thou shouldst not yet doubt religion or the Gods. Thou must perform sacrifices with a will, and practise charity without insolence. Acts in this world have their fruits, and virtue also is eternal. Brahmâ Himself told this unto His sons, as Kâshyapa testifies. Let thy doubt, therefore, O Krishṇâ, be dispelled like mist. Reflecting upon all this, let thy scepticism give way to faith. Slander not God, who is the Lord of all creatures. Learn o know Him. Bow down to Him. Let not thy mind be such. And, O Krishṇâ, never disregard that Supreme Being through whose grace mortal man by piety acquireth immortality."

Draupad still pleaded passionately that it was her husband's duty to regain his kingdom, and Bhîma angrily chimed in, reproaching Yudhishṭhira for their forlorn condition; virtue was not enough, he said; kings must shew strength and fight; let them set forth and do battle, and wrest the sovereignty from Duryodhana. But Yudhishṭhira patiently answered that he deserved blame, and "I cannot reproach thee for torturing me thus by piercing me with thy arrowy words." He had lost his self-control while playing, and had thus brought them to ruin. But he had given his word to abide by the throw of the dice as to exile, and he could not break it; Bhîma should have objected then, if at all. Having given the pledge, he could not violate it. "My promise can never be untrue. I regard virtue as superior to life itself and a blessed state of celestial existence. Kingdom, sons, fame, wealth—all these do not come up even to a sixteenth part of truth." Bhîma, however, would not be persuaded, but continued to argue hotly for battle, till Yudhishṭhira, weary, answered him on lines more suitable to his disposition, and told him that in fighting he would be opposed by Bhîshma, Droṇa, Kripa and Karṇa, and that he could not conquer these. At this Bhîma became silent and depressed, but just then Vyâsa arrived, and taking the young king aside, he bade him send Arjuna in search of weapons from the Gods, and further imparted to him the celestial science of weapons that he might teach it to Arjuna; lastly he advised the brothers to travel from place to place during the absence of Arjuna. [§ 1-36.]

Soon afterwards the young king, calling Arjuna to him, taught him the science given him by Vyâsa, and bade him go to Indra and obtain from him the weapons of the Gods. Taking leave of his brothers and of Krishṇâ, and followed by the blessings of the Brâhmaṇas, the heroic Arjuna set forth alone, and journeyed till he reached the mighty barrier of the Himâlayas, and crossed the snowy range. Reaching Indrakila, he heard a voice cry "stop," and saw a shining ascetic, sitting under a tree. This ascetic bade him throw away his bow, as he had reached a spot where all was peace, but Arjuna refused to disarm himself, though repeatedly pressed to do so. Then the ascetic revealed himself as Indra, and offered him a boon. Arjuna, bowing low, prayed him to give him weapons, but Indra smilingly offered him instead any regions of bliss he might desire. Arjuna refused such gift, his brothers being wanderers in the forest, and, seeing him thus steadfast in duty, Indra answered: "When thou art able to behold the three-eyed, trident-bearing Shiva, the Lord of all creatures, it is then O child, that I will give thee all the celestial weapons. Therefore strive thou to obtain the sight of the highest of the Gods; for it is only after thou hast seen Him, O son of Kuntî, that thou wilt obtain all thy wishes." Then Indra, disappeared, "and Arjuna, devoting himself to asceticism, remained at that spot."

You may remember that after the burning of the forest of Khâṇḍava, Indra had appeared to Arjuna, and had promised to give him celestial weapons after he had obtained the grace of Mahâdeva. That promise was now to be redeemed, but first the condition must be fulfilled. So Arjuna set to work to purify himself, that he might be able to see the great Lord, and at first he took a few leaves and fruits as food, lessening the amount during three months, and then fasted entirely. He was the master of his body, not the servant, as most people are now-a-days, and knew that life is not dependent wholly on food. At last, Mahâdeva took the form of a hunter, a Kirâta, and went to Arjuna, and saw a demon in the shape of a boar, seeking to slay him. Arjuna was going to shoot at the boar, and the Kirâta cried to him to cease, as the boar had been first aimed at by himself. But Arjuna let fly his arrow, and it struck the boar at the same moment as the shaft of the Kirâta. Then Arjuna, telling the Kirâta that the boar was his, threatened to take his life for his breach of forest law, but the Kirâta, smiling, said that *he* had killed the boar and was ready to fight Arjuna. Arjuna drew his great bow and shot at the hunter, but he only smiled and bade him shoot his best. And Arjuna sent at him a shower of arrows, marvelling at his resistance, until his arrows were exhausted, though drawn from the hitherto inexhaustible quivers. Then he rushed at the hunter to strike him down with his bow, but the Kirâta twisted it from his hand. He struck fiercely with his sword; the sword broke. He snatched up rocks and trees; still the hunter bore patiently the shower. Then, rushing at him, he struck him heavy blows with his fist, and the hunter returned the blows and wrestled with him, and at last threw him senseless on the earth. When he regained consciousness, he strove no more, but making a clay image of Mahâdeva, he worshipped it with flowers, and behold! the garland he threw round it appeared on the Kirâta. Then he knew the God and fell at His feet, and Mahâdeva gave him the vision that could see Him, and Arjuna, praying pardon for having fought with Him, and receiving His blessing, was told of his own past and of his divine greatness. Then he prayed for weapons, and Shiva taught him to use His own mighty weapon, the Pâshupata, unknown even to the chief of the Gods, and that weapon "began to wait upon Arjuna as it did upon Shankara." Finally, Shiva bade him go to heaven, and giving him back Gândîva, He disappeared.

As Arjuna still wondered, Indra, Varuṇa, Kuvera and Yama came, surrounded by lesser deities, and Yama gave him his mace, Varuṇa his nooses, Kuvera his favourite weapon that sent the foe to sleep, while, finally, Indra bade him mount his car and ascend to heaven. Then, as the Gods vanished, that splendid chariot came flashing down, and Arjuna, having bathed and prayed, and blessed the holy peak whereon he had lived, mounted the blazing car and drove through space, seeing the self-luminous regions—"so small in consequence of their distance, though very large"—that "are seen from the earth in the form of stars", until he saw shining before him Amarâvatî, the city of Indra. Thereinto he entered and journeyed onwards, surrounded by hosts of celestial beings, till he reached the throne of Indra and bowed before the feet of his divine Father, who raised him and seated him beside himself on his own seat. Indra gave him his thunderbolt and the lightnings, and bade him remain in heaven, and learn of Chitrasena, the king of the heavenly musicians, the Gandharvas, vocal and instrumental music and dancing, *i. e.* the powers of numbers and sounds and rhythmic forms. But though Arjuna obeyed, and learned dutifully all that he was bidden during five years, his heart wearied for his brothers wandering in exile upon earth. But ere he was allowed to leave, he was subjected to a trial, to see if his mind was as pure as his body was strong. Urvashî, a heavenly nymph, was sent to win his love and came to woo him, radiant in dazzling beauty. Now the race of Arjuna had descended from Urvashî, so he bowed before her reverently as the parent of his race, worshipping her as a son his mother. More than this worship he would not give her, and Urvashî was angry, and condemned him to live as a eunuch among women. Arjuna went and told Chitrasena what had occurred, and they went to Indra. Then the God blessed Arjuna, who had "vanquished even Rishis by thy patience and self-control." The apparent curse would be a blessing, for it should take effect during the thirteenth year of exile, through which Arjuna must remain in disguise unrecognised. Indra then sent a great Rishi, named Lomasha, to the earth, to give Arjuna's brothers news of his well-being, and to bid them perform pilgrimages to various sacred shrines. Arjuna, ere he returned to earth, had to destroy certain Asuras, and then he would rejoin his brothers. So Lomasha set out, and went to Yudhishṭhira and his brothers. [§ 37-47.]

You may imagine how delighted the Pâṇḍavas were to hear of their beloved Arjuna and of the success of his mission. Yudhishṭhira gladly agreed to visit the tîrthas, as Indra desired, and they started forthwith on their long round, accompanied by Lomasha. [91-93.] At last, after long wanderings, they reached the Himâlayas, and came to Kailâsa, to the hermitage where Nara and Nârâyana had lived in days of old, and there they rested for awhile, happy and at peace.

One day a north-east wind rose suddenly, and brought a wondrous lotus blossom with a thousand petals and left it on the ground. Draupadî, delighted with its beauty and fragrance, begged Bhîma to find her some more of the same kind, and he, at once, eager to gratify her, set out towards the north-east across the mountains. He fought his way through wild beasts, driving all before him, till he saw a wood of plantain trees that had through it a narrow path, and he directed his steps thither. Now no mortal might pass along that path, so Hanumâna—who, like Bhîma, was a son of the wind-God, and wished to do his brother a service—lay down across the path. Presently up came Bhîma, ready as usual to do battle and shouted loudly to arouse the apparently sleeping monkey. Hanumâna opened his eyes lazily, and complained that Bhîma should awaken him so roughly; moreover, he told the proud young warrior that the path before him was the path of the Gods, and that only by the practice of asceticism might it be trodden. Bhîma demanded who the speaker was, proudly announcing his own name and lineage. "I am a monkey," said Hanumâna indifferently, and he bade him go back lest he should perish. Bhîma haughtily bade him give way, but Hanumâna said he was too ill to rise. Bhîma insisted, and Hanumâna, refusing to move, told Bhîma to pass, moving aside his tail. Then Bhîma caught the tail carelessly in his left hand and pulled, but the tail did not move. He seized it with both hands; it remained steady. Then he pulled and tugged with all his strength, till sweat poured off his body, but still immovable the tail remained. At last, humbled, he bowed before the wondrous monkey, and prayed to know who he was, and learned that he was Hanumâna, the mighty monkey chief, who had befriended Râma, the Avatâra. Then the brothers talked for awhile and Hanumâna, pointing out the way to Bhîma, vanished, while Bhîma went on till he reached a river and lake where the golden lotuses grew in abundance. But as he prepared to gather the lotuses a number of Râkshasas approached, and told him that the lake belonged to Kuvera, and that he must not pick the flowers without asking his permission. Bhîma haughtily refused to ask permission of any one, since a Kshattriya could not beseech, and he plunged forthwith into the lake. Then its guardians attacked him, but he turned on them with his terrible mace and slew them by hundreds, till the survivors fled to Kuvera for aid : but the God, smiling, bade them let Bhîma take for Krishṇâ what flowers he would, and so pacified their anger. Meanwhile Yudhishṭhira and the twins, with Krishṇâ, had followed Bhîma, carried through the air by Ghatotkacha, Bhîma's Râkshasa son, and they all remained for a time at that pleasant spot on the slopes of the Gandhamâdana, expecting the return of Arjuna. Ere long, however, they were sent back to the hermitage of Nara and Nârâyana, and bidden to go thence to two other sacred hermitages. Obediently they set forth, and, following the path traced out for them, they finally—not without adventures on the way—reached Mount Meru, and there abode, longing for Arjuna. Until, one day, as they thought of him, Indra's great car came blazing down from heaven, and there was Arjuna, wearing the diadem and the armour his Father had given him, and, springing to the ground, he bowed down to Dhaumya, Yudhishṭhira and Bhîma. How glad a meeting was that, when Dhananjaya came home again, the years of separation over, and his quest crowned with success. [§ 145-154.]

For four years the brothers abode here, making—with the preceding six—ten years of their exile, and then for another year they wandered through the mountains happily, till they reached the banks of Sarasvatî and there lived for awhile. [§ 175-176.] As the last year of the twelve was passing, they returned to the forest of Kâmyaka and there Shrî Krishṇa came to see them, and, to try him, He bade Yudhishṭhira send an army of the men who were willing to fight for him, led by Balarâma, His own elder brother, to do battle with Duryodhana. But Yudhishṭhira answered steadfastly that they would complete their twelve years in the forest and the one year in disguise, and would then come to Him for help. Associating with Him, how could they do otherwise? "The sons of Pâṇḍu swerve not from the path of truth, for the sons of Prithâ, with their charity and their piety, with their people and their wives, and with their relations, have their protector in Thee." While they were thus talking, the great sage Mârkandeya appeared, and having duly honoured him, Shrî Krishṇa prayed him to tell them of "the eternal rules of righteous conduct by which are guided kings, women and saints." [§ 181, 182.] Then Mârkandeya taught them many things, out of which we can only glance at a few.

Yudhishṭhira asked as to the course of conduct he should follow, and the sage answered: "Be merciful to all creatures, and devoted to their good. Love all creatures, scorning none. Be truthful in speech, humble, with passions under complete control, and always devoted to the protection of thy people. Practise virtue and renounce sin, and worship thou the Pitris and the Gods. And whatsoever thou mayest have done from ignorance or carelessness, wash it off and expiate it by charity. Renouncing pride and vanity, be thou possessed of humility and good behaviour. And subjugating the whole earth, rejoice thou and let happiness be thine. This is the course of conduct which accords with virtue." [§ 190.] On asceticism he taught: "The carrying of three staves, the vow of silence, matted hair on head, the shaving of the crown, covering one's body with bark and deer-skins, the practise of vows, ablutions, the worship of fire, abode in the woods, emaciating the body—all these are useless if the heart be not pure. Those high-souled persons that do not commit sins in word, deed, heart and soul, are said to undergo ascetic austerities, and not they who suffer their bodies to be wasted by fasts and penances. He that hath no feeling of kindness for relatives cannot be free from sin, even if his body be pure. That hard-heartedness of his is the enemy of his asceticism. Asceticism, again, is not mere abstinence from the pleasures of the world. He that is always pure and decked with virtues, he that practises kindness all his life, is a Muni, even though he may lead a domestic life. Such a man is purged of all his sins. Fasts and other penances cannot destroy sins, however much they may weaken and dry up the body that is made of flesh and blood. The man whose heart is without holiness suffers torture only, by undergoing penances in ignorance of their meaning. He is never freed from sin by such acts." So also is charity greater than sacrifices. "He that giveth food to a person that is dying of hunger, and he who, founding a home of charity, establisheth there a person to look after all comers, are both crowned with the merits of all the sacrifices." [§ 199.] Why should any Hindu boy seek teaching from any religion save his own, when such rich stores of noble morality are found in his own sacred books?

In talk such as this, and in the telling and hearing of many priceless stories—such as that of the Brâhmaṇa Kaushika and the virtuous fowler who taught him morality [§ 205-216]—the time passed away. Meanwhile, Shakuni and Karṇa incited Duryodhana to go and visit the Pâṇḍavas, that he might pain them by the contrast between his prosperity and their sad estate. In order that Dhritarâshṭra might not interfere, Karṇa devised the pretext of going to visit their cattle stations in the woods of Dvaitavana, where the princes then were; the king, however, had heard that the Pâṇḍavas were in the neighbourhood of these cattle-stations, and advised Duryodhana to send some one else thither rather than go himself. On the promise of Shakuni, however, that they would not go near the spot where the Pâṇḍavas were living, and on his lying statement that they had "no mind to see the sons of Pâṇḍu," the king reluctantly consented to the expedition, and Duryodhana set out, accompanied by a large army and many followers. They disported themselves in various ways, and counted their cattle at the stations, until they approached the sacred lake of Dvaitavana, where the Pâṇḍavas were residing. As the vanguard of soldiers were about to enter the wood surrounding the lake, some Gandharvas forbade their entry, for the king of the Gandharvas had come thither and had closed the wood against all comers. Then Duryodhana tried to force his way, and a fierce conflict broke out, in which the Kurus were routed, and even Karṇa, who had stood against all assaults, "immovable as a hill," was at last forced to fly. And Duryodhana, who would not fly, was taken prisoner, with Dushâsana and others, and they were led away in chains. Then the routed soldiers of the Kuru army fled to the Pâṇḍavas and prayed them for protection. Bhîma answered sharply and scornfully, refusing all aid, but Yudhishṭhira, saying, "This is not the time for cruel words," rebuked Bhîma, and told him that though disputes might arise in a family, the family honour must be protected when it was assailed by a stranger. Then he bade his brothers arm themselves and go forth and rescue Duryodhana and the other captives.

As the Gandharvas would not release their prisoners, the Pâṇḍavas fiercely attacked them, and they fought until their king and Arjuna coming into conflict, Chitrasena revealed himself as his friend. Then Arjuna asked him why he had assailed Duryodhana, and Chitrasena explained that he had punished him because he had come thither to mock the Pâṇḍavas in their adversity. Somewhat unwillingly Chitrasena consented to lead his captives before Yudhishṭhira, and to allow him to decide their fate after he was made acquainted with their mean wish to glory over him. Then the young king, praising the Gandharvas, at once liberated his relatives, and gently said to the humbled Duryodhana: "O child, never again do such a rash act. O Bhârata, a rash person never attaineth happiness. O son of the Kuru race, blessed be thou, with all thy brothers. Go back to thy capital as it pleases thee, without yielding thyself to despondency or cheerlessness." So spake the gentle king, remembering only that Duryodhana was of his blood and in distress.

Then Duryodhana went away, broken-hearted alike at his defeat and his deliverance, and as he sat, moody and downcast, Karṇa came to him, imagining that he had been victorious, congratulating him that, while he himself had fled, Duryodhana had conquered. Duryodhana soon explained to him the sad truth, and told how their plot had been disclosed and yet Yudhishṭhira had set him free. He was indebted to his persecuted foes for his life. That life was now insupportable to him, and he was resolved to starve himself to death, installing his brother Dushâsana in his place. But Dushâsana flung himself at his brother's feet, weeping, and he swore that he would not rule in his stead, and prayed his brother to turn from his purpose and rule as the head of their race. Then Karṇa spoke again, reproachfully, saying that the Pânḍavas had only done their duty to their king; and Shakuni bade him make friends with the Pânḍavas and give them back their paternal kingdom as a reward. Duryodhana, however, was resolute to die, and sat down on Kusha grass, silent and intent on death. Then the fierce hosts of the Dânavas and Daityas, knowing that in their conflict with the Gods they would be weakened by Duryodhana's death, by magic incantations brought the humbled prince before them, and began to urge on him the folly of suicide. They promised him victory over the Pânḍavas and cheered him with promises of help, telling him that they had obtained him from Maheshvara Himself, and that many heroic Dânavas were born on earth to fight for him. Karṇa would slay Arjuna, and he himself should rule the earth. He was the champion of the Asuras, as the Pâṇḍavas were the champions of the Gods. Duryodhana was then transported back to his place, and, cheered by these promises he rose up and, arraying his army, returned to Hastinâpura. Thence Karṇa set forth, and conquered country after country, bringing them under the rule of Duryodhana, and that prince celebrated a great sacrifice, the Vaishnava, and was hailed as the foremost of kings. His heart, however, was set on performing the Râjasuya sacrifice, which he could not do while Yudhishṭhira was living, and Karṇa, to cheer him, swore that until he slew Arjuna he would not eat meat, nor allow any to wash his feet, nor refuse anything to any one who asked him. [§ 235-255.] Ill did this vow serve him, for when Indra, intent on benefitting Arjuna, came to him and asked him for his natural mail and earrings, he gave them, observing his vow, and thus lost his impenetrable armour. [See the story of Karṇa, §279-309.]

Duryodhana did not cease his plots against the Pâṇḍavas, but no ill that was planned against them took effect. And now the end of the twelve years drew nigh. It was marked by a sharp ordeal of the virtue of Yudhishṭhira. A deer, butting with its horns, caught up the firesticks and the churning staff of a

Brâhmaṇa and carried them away on its antlers. The Brâhmaṇa cried to the Pâṇḍavas to recover for him these implements of sacrifice, and they started in pursuit of the deer. They failed to shoot or overtake it, and at last, losing sight of it, sat down weary and exhausted by thirst. Yudhishṭhira sent Nakula to look for water, who, finding a lake, disregarded a voice that warned him not to drink until he had answered certain questions, and, drinking, fell dead. As Nakula did not return, Sahadeva was sent to seek for him, and met the same fate. Arjuna followed, and Bhîma, and both drank and died. Then Yudhishṭhira himself went to seek, and found his four brothers lying dead on the ground. Overcome with grief, he sought for the enemy that had slain them, and as he began his ablutions in the lake, he heard a voice declaring that the speaker had slain his brothers and repeating the warning given them. Yudhishṭhira enquired, wondering, who he was, and the speaker, a crane, answered that he was a Yaksha, and again bade Yudhishṭhira not take of his water till he had answered his questions. Ever self-controlled, the young king replied that he did not covet what belonged to another, and that he would answer the questions to the best of his ability. The Yaksha then put to him question after question, and Yudhishṭhira answered wisely and well, until at last the Yaksha was satisfied, and granted him the boon of the revival of one of his brothers. Yudhishṭhira chose Nakula, at which the Yaksha remonstrated with him, urging that he should choose Bhîma or Arjuna rather than one of his half brothers. But steadfastly the just king replied that abstention from injury was the highest virtue, and that neither of his father's wives should be left childless. "I desire to act equally towards my mothers. Therefore, let Nakula live." Then the Yaksha said: "Since abstention from injury is regarded by thee as higher than both profit and pleasure, therefore let all thy brothers live, O bull of Bharata's race!" Then the four arose unhurt, and when Yudhishṭhira prayed to know what God was concealed in the crane's form, as it was surely no Yaksha, Dharma, the God of Justice, revealed himself, blessing his noble son. He offered him a boon, and Yudhishṭhira begged that the Brâhmaṇa might have his fire-sticks again. "It was I," said Dharma, "who carried away the fire-sticks as a deer, in order to test thee." And he offered a second boon. Answered Yudhishṭhira: "We have spent these twelve years in the forest and the thirteenth year is come. May no one recognise us as we spend this year somewhere." Dharma granted the boon, and bade them go to Virâta's kingdom, taking what forms they would. And the time having fully come, the five brothers, with Krishṇâ, bade farewell to Dhaumya and the Brâhmaṇas, and, blessed by them, set forth for Virâta. [§ 310–314.]

——:o:——

VIRÂTA PARVA.

Deciding to go to the kingdom of Matsya, ruled over by Virâta, Yudhishṭhira asked his brothers what disguises they would assume; he himself, he said, would go as Kanka, a Brâhmaṇa, skilled in dice, and would act as a courtier. Bhîma answered that he would be a cook and wrestler, Vallava by name; Arjuna, remembering the word of Indra and the curse of Urvashî, said he would disguise himself as a eunuch and live among the queen's women, teaching music and dancing, and his name should be Vrihannalâ. Nakula, under the name of Granthika, would be the keeper of king Virâta's horses, while Sahadeva, as Tantripâla, would tend his kine. Krishṇâ determined to be a Sairindhrî, a superior waiting-maid and companion, and cheerfully prayed Yudhishṭhira not to grieve for her, as the queen would surely cherish her. The young king then sent his priest with the sacred fires to Drupada, and his cars to

Dvârâvati, and his servants to the Pânchâlas, so that none might know of their retreat save Dhaumya only.

Setting forth, the six approached the city of Virâta, and in a huge tree near a cemetery the brothers hid their weapons, hanging a corpse on the tree that none might approach it. Then Yudhishṭhira prayed to the Goddess Dûrgâ, who saves her worshippers from all dangers, and she appeared to him and blessed him, promising him protection and success. Thus blessed, Yudhishṭhira took golden and jewelled dice and entered the court of Virâta, who, struck by by his noble aspect, gave him glad welcome and appointed him as his chief minister and friend. Bhîma appeared, praying to be employed as cook, and Virâta —expressing much doubt as to such office befitting him—agreed to make him superintendent of his kitchen. Krishṇâ, dressing herself humbly, wandered near the palace, and the queen, seeing her, sent for her and asked her who she was; Draupadî answered that she sought for service, but the queen, seeing her marvellous beauty, thought her a Goddess rather than a servant. When Draupadî insisted, the queen replied that she feared to take her into service, for her rare loveliness would win the king's heart; who, indeed, might resist her? But Draupadî told her that she was married to five Gandharvas who ever protected her, and that no man would be allowed to do her wrong. Then Sudeshnâ, the queen, took her into her household with delight, and none guessed who she really was. Now came Sahâdeva, clad as a cowherd, and representing himself as skilled in all cattle-lore, and he was appointed head keeper of Virâta's kine. Next Arjuna appeared, wearing female ornaments, and he prayed that he might be assigned to the princess Uttarâ as teacher of dancing and music; Virâta, declaring that he resembled a warrior and ruler rather than a eunuch, yet tested his skill in the fine arts, and finally sent him among the women to give them lessons. Lastly came Nakula and offered himself as a keeper of horses, and Virâta accepted him and made him his head equerry. Thus did the Pâṇḍavas commence their thirteenth year of exile, and "passed their days of disguise with great composure, notwithstanding their poignant sufferings." [§1—12.]

For ten months they lived in Virâta's court, serving the king and queen, gaining both respect and wealth, and then a menacing storm-cloud arose. The queen's brother, Kichaka, the commander of the army of Virâta, fell madly in love with Krishṇâ's beauty, and would not be gainsaid in his desire to have her as his wife, though she told him of her Gandharva husbands and that to love her was destruction. At last he persuaded his sister Sudeshnâ to send Krishṇâ to his house, under pretext of fetching wine ; in vain Krishṇâ implored her mistress not to send her on such errand, lest Kichaka should insult her and evil should befal. Sudeshnâ, to please her foolish brother, insisted on her going, and Krishṇâ, praying to Sûrya, went forth, accompanied—though she knew it not—by a Râkshasa, appointed by Sûrya to protect her. Kichaka welcomed her with delight and begged her to sit down, but Krishṇâ coldly answered that she came only for wine for her mistress. Kichaka thereupon seized her by the arm, and Krishṇâ, seeking to escape, pushed him violently away and fled to the court, where Yudhishṭhira and Bhîma were seated with the king. Kichaka followed in hot pursuit, and, catching her by the hair, pulled her down and kicked her in the very presence of the king. The Râkshasa flung him senseless to the ground, but what should her husbands do, seeing their beloved thus outraged? As might be expected, Bhîma, furious, was starting up on the verge of self-betrayal but the cold voice of Yudhishṭhira was heard: "Lookest thou, O cook, for trees for fuel? If thou art in need of faggots, then go out and fell trees." Draupadî, striving to keep her promise, addressed king Virâta only, passionately reproaching him for allowing her to be insulted in his presence. Virâta said he knew nothing of the dispute as it had begun elsewhere, but the courtiers began to praise the beauty of Krishṇâ, praise more intolerable to Yudhishṭhira than even the cowardly kick of Kichaka. Yet he lost not his self-control, but, sternly addressing his wife, he said: "Stay not here, O Sairindhrî, but retire to the apartments of Sudeshnâ. The wives of heroes bear affliction for the sake of their husbands, and, undergoing toil in ministering unto their lords, they at last attain to regions where their husbands may go. Thy Gandharva husbands, effulgent as the sun, do not, I imagine, consider this as an occasion for manifesting their wrath, inasmuch as they do not rush to thine aid. O Sairindhrî, thou art ignorant of the timeliness of things, and it is for this that thou weepest as an actress, besides interrupting the play in Matsya's court. Retire, O Sairindhrî! the Gandharvas will do what is agreeable to thee. And they will surely dispel thy woe, and take the life of him that hath wronged thee." Passionately Krishṇâ answered, tortured beyond bearing, and yet striving to keep her pledge: "They of whom I am the wedded wife are, I ween, extremely kind. And as the eldest of them all is addicted to dice, they are liable to be oppressed by all." With this bitter taunt she rushed from the court, and took refuge in the apartments of the queen, where she recounted her wrongs. That night she sought Bhîma and roused him from sleep, and then poured out to him in passionate wailings all her pent-up griefs, blaming Yudhishṭhira as the cause of all. How could she bear to live, seeing her husbands in menial occupations, born princes and rulers of men as they were? And she herself, highborn and a queen, was now a servant, pounding unguents for others, and waiting on them anxiously—and piteously she held out her sweet hands, the soft flesh marked with the pounding-stick. Bhîma, clasping the injured hands tenderly to his face, burst into angry weeping, bewailing the sufferings of his beloved, and praying her to control her grief, as his heart was pierced by his own helplessness to redress her wrongs. For only half a month longer, he cried, be patient, and "thou wilt become the queen regnant of a king." But Krishṇâ, still lamenting, declared that unless Kichaka were slain he would surely outrage her, and then she could not live. If Bhîma would not kill him, then would she, on the morrow, slay herself, and so preserve the chastity her husbands would not protect. Then Bhîma promised to do her will, and bade her make an appointment on the following night with Kichaka in a deserted hall, whither he would come and kill him. Thus did Krishṇâ, and Bhîma kept the appointment in her stead, and, when Kichaka approached with soft words of gallantry, Bhîma answered with mocking praise, and, leaping up, flung himself on his foe and for awhile they wrestled mightily, till the strength of Kichaka failed him and Bhîma crushed him into a shapeless mass. Then he called Krishṇâ and bade her see her slain insulter, and so went his way, and Krishṇâ foolishly cried to the servants, boasting, that her Gandharva husbands had killed her foe. Hearing of his death, Kichaka's relatives came, and, taking his body, seized Krishṇâ also to burn her with him, and she cried out in terror. Bhîma, hearing, slipped out of the palace, and, running to the burning-place, tore up a large tree, and, using it as a mace, slew her assailants and set her free. The outcome of all this was that king Virâta, fearing Krishṇâ, bade his queen ask her to go to some other place, and she, praying for only thirteen days' respite, promised to leave. [§ 13-24.]

Meanwhile the spies of Duryodhana, who had been searching vainly for the Pâṇḍavas, returned to Hastinâpura, confessing the fruitlessness of their errand, but telling that Kichaka, the commander-in-chief of Virâta's army, was dead. Thereupon, a neighbouring king, Susharman, asked Duryodhana's consent and aid in invading Matsya and in seizing king Virâta's cattle, and on the eighth day of the last fortnight of the thirteenth year of the Pâṇḍavas' exile, the Kauravas set forth on this enterprise. Susharman, with his Trigartas, had started on the preceding day. King Virâta with his army, in which were included Yudhishṭhira, Bhîma and the twins, met the Trigartas in battle, and, after a fierce fight, were defeated, Susharman carrying Virâta away on his chariot as a prisoner. Then the four brothers began to fight, and speedily changed the fortunes of the day, Bhîma capturing Susharman and setting Virâta free. Meantime, the Kauravas were seizing the cattle, and the cowherds, flying for assistance, found no one left as leader save a boy-prince, Uttara. The lad proudly said he would go if he had a charioteer, and Draupadî pressed him to take Vrihannalâ, who, she said, had been the charioteer of Arjuna. This was done, and Arjuna, taking the reins as soon as he arrived near the Kurus, urged the horses straight at the foe. Then the boy's courage failed him and he prayed his charioteer to stop; but Arjuna scornfully refused, till poor Uttara sprang from the rushing chariot in terror, throwing away his bow. Indignantly Arjuna flung down the reins and ran after him, and, seizing him by the hair, stopped his flight. "Drive then for me," he cried, and lifted him on to the chariot, and drove quickly to the tree where he had hidden his weapons a year before, bidding Uttara climb into the tree and fetch down the bow of Arjuna that he would find there, as the bows of Uttara would not bear his strength. Once again did Arjuna hold with joy his mighty bow, and, telling Uttara of the weapons and the owners, he finished by saying, "I am Arjuna," and revealing also the identity of his brothers. Then Uttara, rejoicing, lost his fear and took up the reins of the battle-steeds, and Arjuna entered the battle-field with the furious rattling of wheels, the loud blare of his conch, and the crashing twang of the string of Gândîva. Rushing at Karṇa, he first drove that hero, mangled and bleeding, from the field, and then charged on Kripa, destroying his car, so that he also was compelled to leave. Now came Droṇa charging down, and Arjuna saluted him respectfully, refusing to strike unless he struck first: but Droṇa replied with a shower of arrows, and combat raged between preceptor and pupil, until Droṇa's son came to his father's rescue, and Droṇa fled swiftly from the field of battle. Then was Ashvatthâmâ also overcome, and Karṇa, returning, fought once more and was again forced to flee, and at last, as Arjuna was driving before him Dushâsana and his brothers, Bhîshma rushed forward to check him. Mighty was the duel between them, till at last Bhîshma fell unconscious, and his charioteer drove him away from the field. The triumphant Arjuna then put Duryodhana to flight, and at last the Kuru host withdrew vanquished, leaving Arjuna the unchallenged victor of the fray.

Then Arjuna returned to the tree near the cemetery and replaced there his weapons, and again took the reins from Uttara, appearing once more as only Vrihannalâ, the charioteer. Meanwhile Virâta, arriving at his capital after the defeat of the Trigartas, was alarmed to hear that his young son had gone forth to battle with the famous Kuru chiefs and with such an unpromising driver as Vrihannalâ; but Yudhishṭhira consoled him smilingly, telling him that with Vrihannalâ no harm could befall his son. Presently came the news of the victory and of the safety of Uttara, and again Yudhishṭhira remarked that he who had Vrihannalâ for his charioteer must conquer. The king, boasting loudly of his son's exploits, Yudhishṭhira, knowing the time for the revealing had nigh come, said again: "Why should he not conquer that hath Vrihannalâ for his charioteer?" Angry at this repeated praise of a driver, Virâta turned hotly on the disguised prince, asking him whether he compared his son with a eunuch. Yudhishṭhira answered that where Bhîshma and Droṇa and Droṇa's son and Karṇa and Kripa and Duryodhana were leaders, who could fight save Vrihannalâ. "With such a one for his ally, why should not thy son conquer the foe?" Then the king struck Yudhishṭhira furiously in the face, and blood gushed forth; Yudhishṭhira caught it in his hands, and glancing at Draupadî, who was beside him, she quickly brought a golden vessel with water, that the blood might not fall on the ground. At this moment word was brought that Uttara and Vrihannalâ were without, and Virâta bade them enter, but Yudhishṭhira gently whispered to the porter not to allow Vrihannalâ to come in, for if he saw him bleeding, he would slay the king. Thus patient was the noble Yudhishṭhira, even under the intolerable insult of a blow.

Then in came Uttara, and seeing Yudhishṭhira bleeding and learning the cause, he hastily prayed his father to apologise, and the young king pardoned the blow. When the bleeding ceased, Vrihannalâ was allowed to enter, and, having saluted Virâta and his elder brother, he stood silent, awaiting events. The Matsya king, turning to his son, began to applaud him for his marvellous success, but Uttara impetuously answered that he had done nothing; a celestial youth fought for him, and alone had vanquished the great Kuru chiefs; he had disappeared, but would, Uttara thought, return.

At last the happy morning dawned when the thirteenth year of the vow was over, and the five Pâṇḍavas, in white and regal robes, came, blazing with ornaments, into Virâta's council hall, and sat themselves down on the seats reserved for kings. When Virâta came in and saw them thus seated, his wrath blazed up and he angrily reproved the supposed Kanka for his insolence. But Arjuna answered playfully, describing his brother's attainments, and then declaring: "He is no other than the bull of the Kuru race, king Yudhishṭhira the just." Astounded, Virâta asked, if he were indeed Yudhishṭhira, where were his mighty brothers and Draupadî; and Arjuna named them one by one: the cook, the keepers of horse and kine, the Sairindhrî, while he himself was Arjuna. Great was then the joy, and the king worshipped the sons of Pâṇḍu with due honour, offering to Yudhishṭhira his whole kingdom and to Arjuna his fair daughter Uttarâ. Arjuna refused her for himself, since she had ever treated him as a father, but accepted her as wife for his noble son Abhimanyu, the favourite nephew of Vâsudeva. Then to Virâta's court the kings of neighbouring countries and Shrî Krishṇa came, and Subhadrâ and Abhimanyu and many another, and the fair Uttarâ was given to Arjuna's son with many rejoicings, and thus, amid marriage feastings, the thirteen years of exile ended. [§ 25-72.]

——:0:——

CHAPTER VI.

PEACE OR WAR?

At the close of the last chapter we left the princes in the midst of the marriage festivities that succeeded the thirteen years of exile. When these were over, the great question naturally arose: "How to recover the kingdom?" The contract entered into, you will remember, was that at the end of the thirteen years, passed according to the terms, their kingdom should be given back to them. The Pâṇḍavas had manfully carried out their share of the agreement; would Duryodhana perform his? The next section of the "Mahâbhârata," the Udyoga Parva, answers this question, and relates the events which immediately preceded the Great War.

The day after the wedding, the various kings and princes gathered in the council hall of king Vîrâta, who, with Drupada, presided over the royal assembly. After some general conversation, silence fell on the warriors, and they sat waiting, "with their eyes fixed upon Krishṇa," feeling that He, the wise and the lover of the Pâṇḍavas, was the one who could best open the subject they all had at heart. Shrî Krishṇa spoke, briefly narrating the events that had occurred, and pointing out the evil treatment received from boyhood by the Pâṇḍavas from Duryodhana; He bade the kings consider what was for the good of both parties, "consistent with the rules of righteousness and propriety, and what will meet with the approbation of all." "What Duryodhana thinks is not exactly known, nor what he may do." He therefore advised that an ambassador should be sent to beseech them mildly to give half the kingdom to Yudhishṭhira. Valadeva followed, expressing the hope that as Yudhishṭhira was willing to give up half the kingdom, Duryodhana would do the same. He was proceeding to urge that the ambassador should cast the blame of the gambling on Yudhishṭhira and so gain by conciliation; but this was too much for the hot-tempered Sâtyaki, who sprang to his feet and warmly defended Yudhishṭhira, who had only followed the rules of his order; "the means by which I would beseech them would be sharp arrows," cried he. Drupada spoke soothingly, but advised that, having in view the obstinate character of Duryodhana, messengers should be sent to all the surrounding kings, entreating their alliance; this should be done at once, since right-minded persons would grant the request that first reached them; meanwhile let a priest be sent to Dhritarâshṭra as ambassador. This course was approved by Shrî Krishṇa, who thereupon left for Dvârakâ, and Drupada then sent his own priest to the Kuru king, while warriors from all parts began to assemble to espouse the cause of either the Pâṇḍavas or the Kurus. [§ 1-6.]

Now Duryodhana and Arjuna alike desired to secure the alliance of the mighty Keshava, and both, setting out for Dvârakâ, arrived there on the same day and found Shri Krishṇa sleeping. Duryodhana thereupon haughtily seated himself on a handsome seat at the head of the bed, while Arjuna, bowing humbly to the sleeper, stood with joined hands at His feet. As He awaked, His eyes fell first on Arjuna, and, after greeting them, He asked the reason of their visit. Duryodhana answered first, claiming the aid of Shrî Krishṇa in the impending war, and urging compliance with his request on the ground that he was the first to ask assistance. The Lord accepted his assurance that he had arrived first, but said that Arjuna was the first to be seen by Him on awaking; He should therefore help both. He had an army of ten crores of mighty soldiers that He would give to one suppliant; He Himself, unarmed and not fighting, He would give to the other: Arjuna, as the younger, had the right of choice; "you may,

O son of Kuntî, first select whichever of these two commends itself to you." Arjuna, without a moment's hesitation, selected the adorable Krishṇa, whom he loved above all things on earth, while Duryodhana joyfully accepted the powerful army which fell to his share. Valadeva refused to fight on either side, and Duryodhana departed contentedly home with his fighting men, far preferable, to his mind, to Shrî Krishṇa who would not fight. Then Shrî Krishṇa asked His friend why he had selected Himself who would not engage in the battle, and Arjuna answered that he could himself slay his enemies, but he yearned for fame, and that followed Keshava; long had he wished that He should drive his car in battle; "I therefore ask you to fulfil my desire, cherished for a long time." "I will act as thy charioteer," replied the Lord; "Let thy wish be fulfilled." "Then with a glad heart Kuntî's son, accompanied by Krishṇa as well as by the flower of the Dashârha race, came back to Yudhishṭhira." With a glad heart, in truth, for where Shrî Krishṇa was, *there* was victory.

Duryodhana now cleverly stole a march on his opponents, for hearing that Shalya, king of the Mâdras, was on his way to join the Pâṇḍavas, he caused pavilions to be erected on his way where he was splendidly entertained; and when the king asked for the men who had prepared for his coming, believing them to be the servants of the son of Kuntî, Duryodhana presented himself, and, on being offered anything he wished, prayed Shalya to be the leader of his army. Thus entrapped, Shalya was obliged to consent, and went sadly to the sons of Pâṇḍu to tell them of the promise he had been forced to give. Yudhishṭhira at once said he had done rightly, but prayed him, if he drove Karṇa in a combat with Arjuna—as doubtless he would, being equal to Krishṇa as a charioteer—that he would discourage Karṇa and protect Arjuna, damping the spirits of Karṇa by praising his foe. This Shalya promised to do, and departed with his army to Duryodhana. [§ 7, 8, 18.]

Meanwhile the troops were assembling from all sides, till seven Akshauhinis were ranged under the banner of Yudhishṭhira, while no less than eleven were arrayed under Duryodhana. Drupada's priest, arriving at Hastinâpura, pleaded the justice of the Pâṇḍava's cause, pointing out that their paternal property had been usurped by the sons of Dhritarâshṭra, and that when they had made for themselves a new kingdom, that had also been filched from them by fraud. Surely it were better to restore to them their own, as had been promised by the compact, rather than plunge into a ruinous war. Bhîshma supported the arguments of the priest, but was rudely interrupted by Karṇa, and the dispute was waxing hot when Dhritarâshṭra intervened, dismissing the priest courteously, with message that he would send Sanjaya to the sons of Pâṇḍu after due deliberation. Calling Sanjaya, the blind king charged him with many complimentary messages to the injured princes, but promised no redress; and Sanjaya, in delivering these, could only urge peace on general principles. Yudhishṭhira replied somewhat sternly that no one wished for war, but that the king and his sons were forcing it by the denial of justice; let Indraprastha be given to him. Sanjaya urged that it would be better to live on alms than go to war, and Yudhishṭhira appealed to Shrî Krishṇa for his decision. The Lord answered in weighty and impartial words, pointing out that justice lay with the Pâṇḍavas, and reminding Sanjaya of the duty of the Kshattriya. Deeply injured as they were, they yet desired peace, but not at the cost of duty. He concluded by saying He would Himself go to the Kurus to try to bring about an agreement, else would war inevitably ensue. Sanjaya then prayed leave to depart, and was dismissed by Yudhishṭhira with the message: "That desire of thine which torments thy heart, the desire of ruling the Kurus without a rival, is very unreasonable. It hath no justification. As for ourselves, we will never act in such a way as to do any thing that may be disagreeable to thee. O foremost of heroes among the Bhâratas, either give me back my own Indraprastha or fight with me." Then Yudhishṭhira added some loving words to the old king, Bhîshma and Vidura; to Duryodhana he sent a message of forgiveness for all the injuries he had done them and for the insults offered to Krishṇâ, but he insisted that a share of the kingdom must be restored to them; a single province, nay, even five villages, they would accept and end the quarrel. "Let us make peace." Then Sanjaya departed and returned to the court of Dhritarâshṭra. [§ 19-32.]

Long and discordant was the discussion that followed on the return of the herald and his dramatic account of all he had seen and heard. Bhîshma warned the Kurus that Vâsudeva and Arjuna were Nara and Nârâyana, the warrior Gods whom none might hope to defeat, and Droṇa prayed the king to listen to Bhîshma's words. But the king turned from them and enquired as to the forces of the Pâṇḍavas, and then bewailed the coming ruin, though clinging to the counsels of his son. Duryodhana at this encouraged his father, declaring that he felt certain of victory, being himself the greatest of warriors with the mace, having Bhîshma, Droṇa, Ashvatthâmâ, Kripa and Karṇa with him, and his forces exceeding by a third those of the Pâṇḍavas. Again discussion raged, Duryodhana declaring that he would not surrender to the Pâṇḍavas even as much land as a needle's point would cover. Dhritarâshṭra himself at last declared for peace, feeling that war could only end in ruin, but Duryodhana persisted in his resolve to fight, vaunting his own prowess, and declaring that defeat could not crush him. Karṇa supported Duryodhana, boasting that he could himself slay the host of the Pâṇḍavas single-handed, and was thereupon so sharply rebuked by Bhîshma that he, declaring that he laid down his weapons and would not fight until Bhîshma was numbered with the dead, left the court and went to his own abode. Dhritarâshṭra still pleaded with Duryodhana to yield, and when the rest of the counsellors had retired, the blind king appealed to Sanjaya for his opinion as to the result of a struggle; Sanjaya begged that Gândhârî and Vyâsa might be sent for, and then, in their presence, he told the king and his son that Vâsudeva was the Soul of all, the Lord of Time and Death, the increate Creator; "where Krishṇa is success must be." Then the king prayed Duryodhana to yield and take refuge in Keshava, but he declared: "If the divine son of Devakî, united in friendship with Arjuna, were to slay all mankind, I cannot even then resign myself to Keshava." In despair, both father and mother reproached him, and Vyâsa bade the king himself yield to Janârdana, the scene ending with Sanjaya's proclamation of the names of Shrî Krishṇa, and Dhritarashṭra's resolution—alas! not kept—to place himself in the hands of the Eternal One. [§ 46-70.]

Meanwhile the Pâṇḍavas, on their side, were discussing the matter, and Shrî Krishṇa had declared His resolve to visit the Kurus in order to try to avert the impending war. Yudhishṭhira at first objected to His going lest injury should befall Him, but consented on Keshava reminding him that none could stand before him if He arose to slay; He pointed out to Yudhishṭhira that, as a Kshattriya, he could not continue to subsist on alms, and that while He would strive to make peace, He regarded war as certain. And now a surprising thing occured: Bhîma, the warlike and haughty Bhîma, spoke in favour of peace, lest they should become the destroyers of their race—speech "as unexpected as if the hills had lost their weight and fire had become cold." Keshava, laughing, chid him for his gentle mood, declaring that such a frame of mind in him was due to panic, and was "as strange as articulate speech in kine." Bhîma fired up angrily at the taunt, declaring that he felt no fear, but only sought the preservation of the Bhâratas. Then Shrî Krishṇa gently told him that he was all a son of his warrior race should be, but that He had thus spoken because a man would never do rightly who weighed the consequences of his action against his duty. Duty must be done, whatever the apparent result.

It was in the month of Kârtika that Shrî Krishṇa set out on his momentous mission to Hastinâpura, and Dhritarashṭra, hearing of his coming, commanded the most splendid preparations to be made for His reception. On the way Duryodhana, at his order, erected magnificent pavilions at various stages, but Keshava passed by them all, "without casting a single glance" at them. Vidura, indeed, on hearing the directions of the king, remonstrated with him for his insincerity, declaring that he sought to win Keshava by his wealth, a futile hope! Keshava would accept naught save peace, and gifts were of no avail. Duryodhana warmly supported Vidura, holding that this was no fit season for shewing special honour to Keshava, nay, he impiously declared: "this, indeed, is a great resolution which I have formed. I will imprison Janârdana, who is the refuge of the Pâṇḍavas." Horrified, the king protested that Hrishikesha came as an ambassador, while Bhîshma, crying out that Duryodhana would be destroyed, and that he dared not listen to such words, rose and left the palace. [§ 71-87.]

Now Shrî Krishṇa approached Hastinâpura, and all the sons of Dhritarashṭra, save Duryodhana, went out, with Bhîshma, Droṇa and Kripa to bid Him welcome. Having done due homage to the king, He went to the house of Vidura, and there saw the bereaved mother of the Pâṇḍavas. After a natural outbreak of grief, the heroïc spirit of the Kshattriya spoke out in Kuntî, and she sent to each of her sons a stirring message; "The time for that event is come in view for which a Kshattriya woman bringeth forth a son. If you allow the time to sleep without your achieving anything, then, though at present ye are respected by all the world, ye will be only doing that which would be regarded as contemptible. And if contempt touches you, I will abandon you for ever. When the time cometh, even life, which is so dear, should be laid down." Comforting Kuntî, Shrî Krishṇa went on to see Duryodhana and greeted him courteously, but, on being offered food, refused to eat. Duryodhana, speaking gently, but with deceitful purpose, asked why He would not eat, and was answered in measured tones that envoys eat only after their missions were successful, and that Duryodhana might entertain Him when His mission had achieved success. Still pressed, the Lord answered more sternly: "Not from desire, nor from wrath, nor from malice, nor for gain, nor for the sake of argument, nor from temptation, would I abandon virtue. One taketh another's food when that other inspireth love. One may also take another's food when one is in distress. At present, however, O king, thou hast not inspired love in Me by any act of thine, nor have I Myself been plunged into distress. Without any reason, O king, thou hatest, from the moment of their birth thy dear and gentle brothers—the Pâṇḍavas, crowned with every virtue.......Defiled by wickedness, all this food, therefore, deserveth not to be eaten by Me. The food supplied by Vidura alone should, I think, be eaten by Me." Saying thus, Keshava rose and left Duryodhana, returning to the house of Vidura.

Talking that night to Vidura, Shrî Krishṇa explained that He had come to strive to liberate the earth from the meshes of death; He would sincerely strive to bring about peace and to serve both parties; if the Kurus would listen to His words, "words fraught with wisdom, consistent with righteousness and possessed of grave import, then that peace which is My object will be brought about." In the morning He went to the court where the kings were assembled, a splendid array of warrior-chiefs, shining with gold and gems, and all arose in respectful greeting when He, the lotus-eyed, attired in yellow, "like a dark gem mounted in gold," and wearing the blazing jewel Kaustubha, entered the hall. Every eye was fixed on Him and breathless silence prevailed, until His voice, "deep as the roll of clouds in the rainy season," broke the tense stillness. "In order that, O Bhârata, peace may be established between the Kurus and Pâṇḍavas without a slaughter of heroes, I have come hither." He began with pleading soothing words, dwelling on the irresistible strength which would accrue to Dhritarâshṭra if the Pâṇḍavas with his own sons were the defenders of his throne. But if either were slain, where would be his happiness? Let the old love revive with which, as children, he had cherished them. The Pâṇḍavas had kept their pledge during the thirteen years of exile; let the king now keep his. Speaking in their name, He cried: "Knowing that our obedience is due to thee, we have quietly undergone much misery. Behave thou then unto us like a father or brother.........If we go wrong, it is the duty of our father to set us right. Therefore set us on the way, and tread thou also the excellent path of righteousness." Pathetically He reminded Dhritarâshṭra of the wrongs inflicted on the sons of Pânḍu and of their patient endurance and present willingness to forgive. "For the sake of virtue, of profit, of happiness, make peace, O king, and do not allow the earth's population to be slaughtered, regarding evil as good and good as evil. Restrain thy sons, O monarch, who have from covetousness proceeded too far. As regards the sons of Prithâ, they are equally ready to wait upon thee in dutiful service as to fight. That which seemeth to thee to be for thy good, O chastiser of foes, do thou adopt." The silver tones sank into silence, and stillness again brooded over the assembly, the kings thinking "within themselves that there was no man who could dare reply to that speech." At last one Rishi after another addressed Duryodhana, giving him instances of the defeat of those intoxicated by pride. Nârada pleaded long with him, begging him to listen to friends who wished him well, but all was in vain. Then Dhritarâshṭra begged the Lord Himself to strive to persuade his foolish and wicked son, and Keshava, approaching Duryodhana, spoke sweetly to him, praising his good qualities and praying him to turn from his perverse ways and make peace. All would then be happy, and he would obey his father and mother. "Peace with the Pâṇḍavas, O sire, recommends itself to thy father. Let it therefore, O chief of the Kurus, recommend itself to thee." To follow unrighteousness was to court ruin. Let not his relatives and the chiefs who followed him be slain. "Let not people say that thou art the exterminator of thy race and the destroyer of its achievements." He might be lord paramount with the consent and support of the Pâṇḍavas. "Making peace with the Pâṇḍavas and acting according to the counsels of thy friends, and rejoicing with them, thou art sure to obtain what is for thy good for ever and ever." Bhîshma followed, praying Duryodhana not to sink his father and mother in an ocean of grief, and Droṇa pleaded, and Vidura and Dhritarâshṭra himself, and again Bhîshma and Droṇa, all with loving words and gentle urgings, but all in vain. Duryodhana spoke fiercely in reply, declaring himself faultless, and again saying that while he lived, "even that much of our land which may be covered by the point of a sharp needle shall not, O Mâdhava, be given by us unto the Pâṇḍavas." Then replied Keshava sternly: "Wishest thou for a bed of heroes? Verily thou shalt have it with thy councillors." "Thou art not, O sinful man, willing to give them their paternal share in the kingdom although they are begging it of thee. Thou shalt have to give it to them when, divested of prosperity, thou shalt be laid low." At this Duryodhana, infuriated, rose and left the court, rudely disregardful of his elders, and followed by his brothers and those on his side. Then Vâsudeva advised the king to arrest Duryodhana, Karṇa, Shakuni and Dushâsana and to bind them and hand them over to the Pâṇḍavas, so that the whole Kshattriya race should not be slain. But Dhritarâshṭra, as a last resort, sent for Gândhârî and prayed her to speak to their headstrong son, and she summoned Duryodhana back to the court, who came, flushed with anger. Gently the mother pleaded with him, but where the golden tongue of Shrî Krishṇa had failed, how should even a mother's voice prevail? Duryodhana again left the court in a rage, without a word of answer, without a gesture even of reverence, and plunged headlong into his mad plot for seizing the divine Krishṇa. Sâtyaki guessed at his wicked plan and warned Keshava, Dhritarâshṭra and Vidura, saying that in desiring to seize the lotus-eyed, they were "like idiots and children desiring to seize a blazing fire with their garments." Keshava bade the king let Duryodhana try his worst, promising that He would do no wrathful act, and Duryodhana and his brothers and supporters being called back into the court, his father and Vidura sternly told him of Keshava's might and that none might seize Him by force against His will. Then Keshava, addressing Duryodhana, said: "From delusion, O Suyodhana, thou regardest Me to be alone, and it is for this, O thou of little understanding, that thou seekest to make Me a captive after vanquishing Me with violence. Here, however, are all the Pâṇḍavas and all the Vrishnis and Andhakas. Here are all the Adityas, the Rudras, and the Vasus, with all the great Rishis!" And as the mighty One laughed at His puny foe, lo! from out His body issued myriad forms of Gods and formed a blazing halo round Him, and Arjuna stood on His right and Râma on His left, with the four Pâṇḍavas behind Him, and the roll of drums thundered through the hall and flowers fell as rain. And as all wondered, the divine glory vanished, and Keshava left the court, finding outside His white chariot awaiting Him. Then Dhritarâshṭra, following, addressed Him sadly, protesting his powerlessness to control his sons, and Keshava answered sternly and shortly, addressing the great chiefs and the king: "Ye have yourselves witnessed all that has happened in the assembly of the Kurus, how the wicked Duryodhana, like an uneducated wretch, left the court in anger, and how king Dhritarâshṭra also describeth himself to be powerless.

With the permission of you all, I will now go back to Yudhishṭhira." With a grave salute, Keshava ascended the chariot, and went to visit Kuntî, who again sent fiery messages to her sons, inviting them to battle. He then called Karṇa and took him with Him a brief way, and, after dismissing him, drove away, leaving the Kurus to their doom. The last throw had been made for peace, and was lost. War was now inevitable. [§ 87-136.]

Bhîshma and Droṇa, left behind, once more besought Duryodhana to make peace, assuring him of their fealty but pathetically bewailing their enforced combat with the Pâṇḍavas, of whom, said Droṇa, Arjuna was dearer to him than his own son. They were old; their lives were over. But he was still young, and was flinging away friends, kingdom and life. [§ 137-138.] It is sometimes asked, why should not Bhîshma and those like-minded with him have gone to the Pâṇḍavas, and fought on the side where lay their hearts and the blessing of the Gods? Bhîshma above all, devoted to Shrî Krishṇa, how could he lift bow against Him? Bhîshma, whose life was the symbol of duty, righteousness and justice, how could he war against the side that embodied these, and on the side arrayed against them? Yet Bhîshma, as the incarnation of duty, never shone more brightly than in these closing scenes of his life. And Droṇa? He who had trained Arjuna, who loved none as he loved him, why should he go forth to do battle with him? Because under all trials, in all the circumstances of life, in face of heart-break and death, duty must be done. And for the Kshattriya, duty of combat for his king, for the cause of his country, was the supreme law of life. The bodies worn by Bhîshma and Droṇa owed allegiance to Dhritarashṭra and his sons; they were his subjects, his warriors, his councillors; they had lived, worked, fought in his service all his life through. Not for pain and suffering, not for broken heart and ruined life, could Bhîshma and Droṇa leave duty. They must pay with their bodies the debt those bodies owed. Their love, their hopes, their reverence, were with Shrî Krishṇa and His friends, but their bodily strength, their warrior arms, their skilled brains, their might as leaders, lay at the feet of the king to whom they had sworn allegiance. Not for them to judge of the right or wrong of the quarrel when war outbroke; theirs to fight where their karma had placed them. So they got them ready for the battle, to fight outwardly against the Lord they loved, hoping, it may be, that in the struggle a bolt from Him might lay them low, that they might die of the wounds of love.

What was happening between Shrî Krishṇa and Karṇa, as they drove a short way together? A strange scene truly, the roots of which were in the past. We remember that Kuntî had been given a mantra by Durvâsa which enabled her to summon any God to give her a son. Soon after receiving this mantra, ere she met Pâṇḍu, in girlish curiosity and folly, to try its force, she had repeated the mantra with the name of Sûrya, the Sun-God. On his appearing, she was frightened, and begged him earnestly to depart, and not compel her to bear a son; she pleaded her childish foolishness and begged forgiveness, but the force of the mantra bound the Sun-God, and a glorious child was born of her, clad in natural armour, radiant and strong. Left by his mother at Sûrya's command, he was found by Râdhâ, the wife of the charioteer Adhiratha, and she took compassion on him, and brought him up as her own son. This was Karṇa. [*Adi Parva*, § 302-308.] Shrî Krishṇa now reminded him of his real mother Kuntî, whose husband Pâṇḍu was legally his father. He was thus, said Keshava, the eldest brother of the Pâṇḍavas, and He would now take him to them and tell the story of his birth. Gladly would they bow down to him as the rightful monarch; he should be crowned king, and all the Pâṇḍavas and their hosts, including Himself, would follow him; the sovereignty of the earth should be his, and the love of his younger brothers. Gently but steadily, Karṇa put away the proffered rule and happiness; Kuntî had abandoned him, and, though of right the eldest son of Pâṇḍu, he could not take up the broken bonds of kinship. He owed everything to the Suta Adhiratha and his wife Râdhâ, care in infancy, protection in childhood, fatherly guidance and training. His wives were of Adhiratha's choice; sons and grandsons had been born to him. By every tie of family, love, fidelity, he was bound to his adopted kin and to their order. To Duryodhana also, who gave him a kingdom, he was bound by gratitude; Duryodhana was going into this war depending on him, and he was selected to meet Arjuna in single combat. Above all, the Pâṇḍavas must not know the story of his birth, else would they never fight against him or accept the kingdom. Besides, were the kingdom his, he would give it to Duryodhana. Yudhishṭhira was worthy to be king, and the kingdom was already practically won. The battlefield would be a sacrificial platform, where the leaders would be the priests, the warriors the offerings, arrows the sacrificial ladles. There would he himself be slain by Arjuna while Bhîma would slay Dushâsana and Duryodhana. For all the harsh words he had spoken to the sons of Pâṇḍu he was consumed with repentance. With one prayer he ended: "Oh! let this swelling host of Kshattriyas perish by means of weapons on that most sacred of all spots in the three worlds, Kurukshetra, O Keshava! O Thou of eyes like lotus-leaves, accomplish on this spot what Thou hast in Thy mind, so that, O Thou of Vrishni's race, the whole Kshattriya order may attain to heaven." Graciously the Lord answered him that with the great battle the ages Krita, Treta and Dvâpara would vanish, and He bade him go to Bhîshma, Droṇa and Kripa and say to them the time was fair and pleasant; seven days thence was the day of the new moon; then let the battle join, and the warriors, "obtaining death by weapons, will attain to an excellent state." For thus, in the counsels of the Gods, was the great Kshattriya order to pass from the earth, leaving it to the Kali Yuga. Then Karṇa worshipped Keshava, and relating a vision in which he had seen the Pâṇḍavas truimphant and only Asvatthâmâ, Kripa and Kritavarman as survivors of Duryodhana's army, he spoke his last words to Shrî Krishṇa. "If, O Krishṇa, we come out with life from this great battle that will be so destructive of heroic Kshattriyas, then, O Thou of mighty arms, may we meet here again. Otherwise, O Krishṇa, we shall certainly meet in heaven. O sinless one, it seemeth to me now that there only it is possible for us to meet." "Having spoken these words, Karṇa tightly pressed Mâdhava to his bosom. Dismissed by Keshava, he then descended from the car. And riding on his own car, decked with gold, Râdhâ's son, greatly dejected, came back." Such was the last interview between Shrî Krishṇa and Karṇa, till they met face to face on the field of Kurukshetra. [§ 139-142.]

One other painful interview had Karṇa to face—one with his own mother. Kuntî sought him, and prayed him to take his rightful place as Kshattriya and Pâṇḍava, and to be united with Arjuna as was Keshava with Balarâma. Her pleading was reinforced by a voice issuing from the Sun: "The words said by Prithâ are true. O Karṇa, act according to the words of thy mother. O tiger among men, great good will result to thee if thou fully followest those words." But "Karṇa's heart did yet not waver, for he was firmly devoted to truth," and he again refused to desert his friends in the hour of their danger. "This is the time when all those that have been supported by Dhritarâshṭra's sons should exert themselves for their masters. I shall certainly act for them, reckless of even my life. Those sinful men of unsteady heart, who, well-fed and well-furnished by their masters, undo the benefit received by them when the time cometh for paying back those benefits—verily, those sinful men, those faithless servants of kings, those thieves of their master's cakes, have neither this nor the other world." One pledge, however, Karṇa made; in the coming battle he would not slay Yudhishṭhira, Bhîma, nor the twins; only against Arjuna would he fight to the death, to slay him or by him to be slain. [§ 143-145.]

Arrived at Upaplavya, where the Pâṇḍavas were staying, Shrî Krishṇa related to them all that had occurred, concluding by saying that the kings allied with the Kurus had already marched to Kurukshetra, and that nothing remained save to fight. [§ 146-149.] Then discussion arose as to who should lead the whole army, the separate divisions, or Akshauhinis, being severally assigned to Drupada, Virâta, Dhrishṭadyumna, Shikhaṇḍin, Sâtyaki, Chekitâna and Bhîma. The various chiefs gave their opinions in turn, and the final decision was referred to Shrî Krishṇa, who named as commander-in-chief the sacrifice-born Dhrishṭadyumna, the foretold slayer of Droṇa. Then marched forth the great host in order, and encamped on the field of Kurukshetra. Of the opposing Kaurava host Bhîshma was made generalissimo, Karṇa, according to his promise, refusing to fight until Bhîshma was slain. [§ 150-198.] With the clash of arms, the beating of drums, the blare of conches, concludes the Udyoga Parva.

We open the Bhîshma Parva, the Parva that tells of the ten days' fighting of Bhîshma, and contains the immortal, the incomparable, *Bhagavad Gîtâ.*

Vyâsa, coming to the blind king Dhritarâshṭra, offered him sight to behold the battle; but Dhritarâshṭra, shrinking from the seeing of slaughter, the Rishi bestowed on Sanjaya celestial vision, that he might describe to the king all that occurred, whether it happened by day or night or was only thought of in the mind. As to the result of the combat, victory, said the sage, "is there where righteousness is." [§ 1-2.] Truly, however wrong may seem to triumph, as it did against the Pâṇḍavas, truth and justice ultimately carry all before them. Outnumbered by a third, the Pâṇḍavas were yet destined to triumph, according to words spoken by Brahmâ in another combat and quoted by Arjuna as the armies were arrayed for battle. "They that are desirous of victory do not conquer by might and energy so much as by truth, compassion, righteousness and energy. Discriminating then between righteousness and unrighteousness, and understanding what is meant by covetousness, and having recourse to exertion, fight without arrogance, for victory is there where righteousness is." And Nârada had said: "There is victory where Krishṇa is." Then Shrî Krishṇa bade Arjuna hymn Dûrgâ, the Giver of victory, and he sang to Her who lifts Her worshippers above all defeat and misery, above all calamities. And the mighty Goddess appeared and promised Arjuna that he should conquer his foes, and Arjuna mounted on his chariot with Keshava as his charioteer. [§ 21-23.]

Drawn up by Keshava between the two armies ere the flight of arrows began, Arjuna's lion-heart faltered, and he sank despondent on the floor of his car. Not from fear, or the sight of his foes in serried array, not from terror of death nor of warrior's charge, failed that heroic heart. But for the impending slaughter of relatives, of comrades, of boyhood's dear companions, and the friends of maturer years; for Bhishma, more than father, for Droṇa, preceptor beloved. The iron heart of the warrior broke with anguish; "I will not fight!" he cried, and cast away his bow. Then the Lord, to cheer him, spake the wonderful Song, the Song Celestial, that, uttered five thousand years ago, has since echoed from heart to heart, sweetest and loftiest of all teaching given to those who love the Lord. Shrî Krishṇa spake the *Bhagavad Gîtâ*. [§ 25-42.]

And now occurs a strange thing. As the armies are ready to engage, king Yudhishṭhira throws down his weapons, puts off his armour, and with joined hands approaches the hostile force. Alarmed, Arjuna leaps down to follow him, and the other brothers and Keshava and all the kings follow him, and they call aloud anxiously, asking him whither he goes. Only Keshava says, smiling, "His object is known to me," and explains it to the puzzled chiefs. From the enemy arise shouts of derision; he is afraid, he seeks shelter! Then all is silent, and Yudhishṭhira, unarmed, presses through the armed ranks of his foes till he reaches Bhîshma, and clasping his feet, he says: "I salute thee, O invincible one! With thee will we do battle. Grant us thy permission in this matter. Give us also thy blessing." And Bhîshma blessed him with the promise of victory, and bade him ask what boon he would: "Bound am I to the Kauravas by wealth. Battle excepted, what dost thou desire?" Then Yudhishṭhira asked who might conquer him in battle, and Bhîshma replied that none might defeat him so long as he fought. How then could he be slain? "The time also of my death is not yet come," answered Bhîshma. "Come to me once again." Then Yudhishṭhira paid due homage to Droṇa, who told him he could only be slain when he cast away his arms on hearing evil tidings and withdrew himself in Yoga meditation. Also to Kripa and to Shalya he offered similar homage and received their blessings, and then returned to his own army, while all men applauded the noble courtesy of the sons of Pâṇḍu. [§ 43.]

Then the battle outbroke in fury, and Bhîshma carried all before him, and many a great warrior fell. Then was slain young Uttara, son of Virâta, and his elder brother, Sveta, furious with wrath, charged on the enemy and drove them headlong, till Bhîshma rushed against him, and after long combat between the heroes Sveta fell, his death closing the day's struggle. [§ 44-48.] On the following day, as the Pâṇḍavas were flying before Bhîshma, Arjuna angrily told Keshava to drive him against that mighty warrior, and the flashing chariot with its milk-white steeds thundered across the field, and Bhîshma and Arjuna met in deadly fray. For hours they fought, neither having the advantage, while many a deadly combat of heroes took place around, till Bhîshma turned aside to rescue his troops assailed by Bhîma, and, his charioteer being slain, his steeds rushed from the field. Then Arjuna, set free, after saving from imminent danger his heroic son Abhimanyu, raged over the field, scattering all before him, until sundown came, and darkness saved the routed Kurus from his arrows. On the third day, the Kurus were again flying from their foes, when Bhîshma, stung to fury at the sight, charged down upon the Pâṇḍavas and changed the fortune of the day. Then, as the Pâṇḍavas in turn gave way, Keshava turned the silvery steeds against Bhîshma's onslaught, and brought Arjuna to meet the grandsire again. Arjuna then attacked his beloved enemy, but with mildness, hating his task, till Keshava, to sting him to exertion, called His mighty discus, and whirling it on high, leapt from the chariot and rushed at Bhîshma, who cried aloud in joyous welcome, "Slain here by thee, O Krishṇa, great will be my good fortune both in this world and the next." But Arjuna, shamed as he was meant to be, ran after Keshava, and flinging his arms round Him, dragged Him back, promising to fight more energetically, and Keshava took up the reins again, and the battle raged furiously till set of sun, Arjuna driving all before him. [§ 48-59.] Thus for day after day the combatants fought, and success seemed sometimes on one side and sometimes on the other, yet wherever Bhîshma turned, the tide of battle flowed against the Pâṇḍavas. Ten thousand men a day he destroyed; he "blazed up like a fire in the midst of a forest and consumed his foes." [§ 60-99.]

On the ninth day the mighty warrior was even more invincible than before, and it seemed as though the lot of battle were to be finally cast against the Pâṇḍavas. As evening was approaching Keshava once more hotly rebuked Arjuna, who was fighting half-heartedly, and who again, at His bidding, attacked unwillingly the great chief; and once more, as though hopeless of stimulating His friend in any other way, He leapt from the chariot with only whip in hand, and rushed through the battle, though but robed in yellow silk, on Bhîshma. Once more that noble warrior welcomed death threatening from that beloved hand: "Strike me as thou pleasest, for I am thy slave, O sinless one!" And once more, Arjuna, shame-stricken, checked Shrî Krishṇa's onset: "O Thou of mighty arms, stop! O Keshava, it behoveth Thee not to make those words false which Thou hadst spoken before, I will not fight: O Mâdhava, people will say that Thou art a liar. All this burden resteth upon me. I will slay the grandsire. I swear, O Keshava, by my weapons, by truth and by my good deeds, that, O slayer of foes, I will do all by which the destruction of my foes may be achieved." Mâdhava wrathfully remounted the car, and still Bhîshma carried all before him till night fell on the ninth day of combat.

That night Yudhishṭhira so lamented the slaughter,

that Keshava offered to throw aside his promise and Himself slay Bhîshma; but the young king, abiding firm by truth, refused to allow Keshava to falsify His words. Had not Bhîshma promised them counsel? He might tell them how to compass his own death. Let them all go to Bhîshma, and ask his advice. And a bitter cry ended the speech: "We were children and orphans. By him were we reared. O Mâdhava, him, our aged grandsire, I wish to slay—him, the sire of our sire! Oh! fie upon the profession of a Kshattriya!" Keshava approved the proposal, and casting aside their armour and weapons, Keshava and the five sons of Pâṇḍu went on, to modern view, the strangest of errands, to ask Bhîshma how they might slay him in battle. Bhîshma gave them warm welcome and Yudhishṭhira gently put before him the request to advise them how to bring about his own defeat and death. Bhîshma answered that while he lived they could not conquer, but that they might strike him as they would. Yudhishṭhira declaring that they could not slay him, Bhîshma calmly gave them his own death-warrant; for to men like Bhîshma there is only one will, the will of the Supreme Lord, and they hold themselves as His, without anxiety or wish of their own. There was a mighty warrior among them named Shikhaṇḍin; he had been a female, and against such a one he, Bhîshma, would not fight; let Arjuna place Shikhaṇḍin before him, and Bhîshma would not strike; then let Arjuna "quickly pierce me on every side with his shafts." At this Arjuna burst out, "burning with grief and his face suffused with shame." "How, O Mâdhava, shall I fight in battle with the grandsire who is my senior in years, who is possessed of wisdom and intelligence, and who is the oldest member of our race? While sporting in days of childhood, O Vâsudeva, I used to smear the body of this high-souled and illustrious one with dust by climbing on his lap with my own filthy body. O elder brother of Gada, he is the sire of my sire Pâṇḍu. While a child, climbing on the lap of this high-souled one, I once called him father. 'I am not thy father, but thy father's father, O Bhârata!'—even this is what he said to me in my childhood. He who said so, oh! how can he be slain by me? Oh! let my army perish. Whether it be victory or death that I obtain, I will never fight with that high-souled person. What dost thou think, O Krishṇa?" Gravely and gently the Lord answered that having vowed to slay Bhîshma he could not, as a Kshattriya, abstain from doing so. It was the condition of victory. "O Dhananjaya, this is the eternal duty sanctioned for the Kshattriyas, that they should fight, protect subjects, and perform sacrifices, all without malice." Having settled all with Bhîshma's permission, the Pâṇḍavas and the Lord retired, to await the dawning of the tenth day of battle, the day of sacrifice on which Bhîshma was to be the glorious victim and Arjuna the sacrificing priest. [§ 100-108.]

At sunrise Shikhaṇḍin's division advanced against Bhîshma, and Bhîshma charged against it, but mockingly refused to aim a blow at its leader, since he was still the woman God had made him. Greater than ever shone forth Bhîshma on that last day of battle, crimsoning all around him like the setting sun. None could stand before him save Arjuna, with his white steeds that were as the steeds of Death, and Shikhaṇḍin whom he would not smite. Disregarding Shikhaṇḍin, he shot only at Arjuna. As sunset drew near, Bhîshma, knowing that death might not touch him save by his own will, spoke within himself: "I should now, however, wish my own death, this being the proper hour." Then the Rishis and the Vasus, who watched the battle, cried to him: "That which has been resolved by thee is approved by us also, O son. Act according to thy resolution, O king. Withdraw thy heart from battle." And a sweet breeze breathed fragrantly on the hero, and a flowery shower fell. In vain arrows rained on him from all other combatants; he stood unmoved. But for Arjuna's shafts his will made way, and they pierced him through and through. Smiling, he said to Dushâsana: "These arrows coursing towards me in one continuous line, whose touch resembleth that of heaven's bolt, have been shot by Arjuna......Save the heroic wielder of Gândîva, the ape-bannered Jishnu, even all other kings united together cannot cause me pain." The arrowy shower continued, till "there was not in Bhishma's body space of even two fingers' breadth that was not pierced with arrows." And a little before sunset he fell from his chariot, his head to the east, so transfixed with arrows that his body could not touch the ground, and he lay, upheld by shafts, on a bed of arrows. While falling, he marked that the sun was in his southern path, and heavenly voices cried: "Why, oh! why should Gangâ's son, that foremost of all warriors with weapons, yield up his life during the southern declension?" And he cried aloud: "I am alive!" and suffered not his senses to depart. Then Gangâ sent the great Rishis to him in swanlike forms, and they repeated the same question. And Bhîshma said: "I will never pass out as long as the sun is in the southern path. Even this is my resolve. I will proceed to my own ancient abode when the sun reacheth the northern path.......The boon that was granted to me by my illustrious sire, that my death would depend on my own wish, oh! let that boon become true. I will hold my life, since I have control in the matter of laying it down."

Then the roar of battle ceased and all men laid down their weapons, and the very sun grew dim, and earth bewailed his fall. The kings of both armies, putting off their armour, approached him reverently and did him homage, and he greeted them with blessings. Then, his head hanging down, he asked for a pillow, but when they brought soft and delicate pillows, he put them aside, laughing: "These, ye kings, do not become a hero's bed." And seeing Arjuna standing by, he said: "O Dhananjaya, O thou of mighty arms, my head hangeth down. O sire! give me a pillow, such as thou regardest to be fit." Then Arjuna, blinded with tears, took three keen shafts and blessed them with mantras to support Bhîshma's head, and the hero smiled, well-pleased: "Thou hast given me, O son of Pâṇḍu, a pillow that becometh my bed.........Even thus, O mighty armed one, should a Kshattriya, observant of his duties, sleep on the field of battle on his bed of arrows." And he bade them dig a ditch round the place where he lay, and cease from fighting. Refusing the offices of the physicians, he lay and turned himself to prayer. On the morrow, tortured by his wounds and burning with fever, he asked for water; but, rejecting what was brought, he again called Arjuna: "Covered all over with thy shafts, my body is burning greatly. All the vital parts of my body are in agony. My mouth is dry. Staying as I am with body afflicted with agony, give me water, O Arjuna. Thou art a great bowman. Thou art capable of giving me water duly." Then Arjuna drew Gâṇḍîva and shot an arrow mantra-directed, and where it pierced the earth pure water burst forth, and he gave of it to Bhîshma to drink. Then Bhîshma, refreshed, praised him, and calling Duryodhana, once more bade him make peace, since none might vanquish Arjuna with Keshava at his side. "Desist even now!" he said, and was silent, and "though his vital parts were burning with the arrow-wounds, yet, prevailing over his agonies, he applied himself to yoga." Presently, when all had gone, Karṇa came, tear-choked, and fell at his feet: "O chief of the Kurus, I am Râdhâ's son, who, while before thine eyes, was everywhere looked at by thee with hate." Then Bhîshma opened his pain-glazed eyes, and threw his arm round Karṇa, and spoke to him loving words. "O thou that resemblest a very God, among men there is none like to thee. For fear of intestine dissensions, I always spoke harsh words about thee." And he praised him as equal to Arjuna, and bade him unite with his own brothers, the heroic sons of Pâṇḍu. But this Karṇa could not do: to the end he must fight the Pâṇḍavas. "Grant me thy permission, O hero. I will fight. Even this is my wish. It behoveth thee to forgive me also any harsh words that I may at any time have uttered against thee, or any act that I may have done against thee from anger or inconsiderateness." Then Bhîshma gave him leave. "Fight, moved by the desire of heaven. Without anger and without vindictiveness serve thou the king, according to thy power and thy courage, and observant of the conduct of the righteous." In peace the old foes parted and Karṇa went back to Duryodhana, leaving Bhîshma to pay his last debt of agony with the body that, though rightly, had yet fought against righteousness, waiting patiently the appointed ending, the willing victim on his couch of pain.

—:o:—

CHAPTER VII.

THE SIN OF YUDHISHṬHIRA.

Sadly withdrawing from Bhîshma, leaving him to hold death at bay, the kings prepared to resume the interrupted battle. But who should replace the grandsire, the hero, the mightiest warrior of the Kuru hosts? All hearts turned towards one man, the man who for ten days had stood aside from battle, and one cry arose, "Karṇa! Karṇa!" Karṇa was willing to fight, but first sought Bhîshma's permission, who bade him go into the battle, and Duryodhana prayed him to lead the army in Bhîshma's stead unless he thought some other chief should be chosen. Karṇa advised the king to anoint as commander-in-chief the one who had taught them all the use of weapons and whom therefore all would cheerfully follow, Droṇa the great preceptor. All the kings hailed the suggestion with delight, and Droṇa, accepting the leadership was duly installed, and set the army in array for the eleventh time against the foe. The events of his leadership are narrated in the Droṇa Parva. Ere recommencing the battle, Droṇa offered Duryodhana a boon, and he chose the capture of Yudhishṭhira, craftily saying that the slaughter of the young king would leave his brothers in his stead who would avenge him, but his capture alive would keep them in obedience to their elder, and he could again exile them by another victory at dice. Droṇa declared that Yudhishṭhira could only be captured by drawing Arjuna away from his side, and the Pâṇḍavas, hearing of this plot, arranged their own plans to counteract it, Arjuna swearing that Droṇa should not seize Yudhishṭhira while he was living, although he could not himself slay his teacher. With this centre of combat, the capture of Yudhishṭhira, the struggle recommenced. Many deeds of prowess were done on both sides, Abhimanyu, Arjuna's glorious son, a mere boy, fighting desperate duels with Paurava, Jayadratha and Shalya, while Bhîma's Râkshasa son, Ghatotkacha, performed prodigies of valour. Meanwhile Droṇa, drawn by splendid chesnut steeds, had made a tremendous onslaught in the direction of Yudhishṭhira, and trampling down all opponents he reached the car of the young king. Shouts of victory from the Kurus rent the air, as they thought Yudhishṭhira was captured; but lo! the white steeds of Arjuna, guided by Keshava, come flashing across the field with the rattle of thunder, and Ḍhananjaya routs them, driving them in every direction, as the sun sets on the eleventh day. [§ 1-16.]

During that night six brothers, headed by Susharman, king of the Trigartas, took a solemn oath to slay Arjuna, or to die in battle against him. They then challenged Arjuna, who, bound by his vow never to refuse a challenge, prayed the king's permission to go, leaving him in the charge of Satyaki; Yudhishṭhira bade him go against the hosts of these brothers, called Samsaptakas—men sworn to conquer or die—and he turned towards the quarter where they were arrayed. As Arjuna became engaged in fierce conflict, Droṇa rushed upon Yudhishṭhira, and, after furious battling round the young king, his guards broke, and he fled before his ancient teacher. Bhîma then rushed into the fray, but despite all his efforts, and a desperate conflict with an elephant that was trampling down men, horses and chariots, the Pâṇḍava host was giving way. Between the Samsaptakas on one side and his struggling forces on the other, "Arjuna's heart was divided in twain," and he scarce knew which way to turn. But resolving first to have done with his challengers, he charged furiously upon them and annihilated them, and then the silvery steeds whirled him like lightning against the division of Droṇa. Charging, he met the elephant carrying Bhagadatta that had caused such slaughter, but his car, guided by Keshava, evading the elephant's rush, he would not slay it from behind but turned again to face it. Then Bhagadatta flung a weapon at Arjuna, and Keshava, throwing Himself in front of His friend, received the bolt upon His breast, and it became there a triumphal garland. But Arjuna reproached his divine Charioteer for His interference, only permissible were he overcome, thinking himself shamed by such defence. Then Shrî Krishṇa gently told him that this weapon, the Vaishṇava, might be turned aside by none save by Himself, for it was His own, granted once in boon to the Earth for her son, from whom Bhagadatta had received it. Invincible while he held it, he had now thrown it away, and Arjuna could slay both monarch and elephant. When at last night fell and closed the twelfth day's battle, the Pâṇḍavas held the field and Droṇa's promise to seize Yudhishṭhira was yet unfulfilled. [§ 17-32.]

The thirteenth day was the day for the return of Varchas to Svarga—he who was born as Abhimanyu of Shrî Krishṇa's sister Subhadrâ—and the glory of the day was won by this heroic boy. Scarce out of childhood, but sixteen years of age, he fought like a veteran and carried all before him. Arjuna was again challenged and drawn away, and his young son was bidden by Yudhishṭhira to lead the charge against Droṇa's army, advancing in a circular form that only Arjuna, Keshava, Praddyumna and this lad knew how to break. They would all follow him, but only he could break the array. Abhimanyu joyfully accepted the task, proud of his father and his mother's brother, and, vowing in their names to conquer, he bade his reluctant charioteer drive him against the foe, "like an infant lion assailinga herd of elephants." The fury of his onset broke the array, and he fought single-handed against Droṇa and his son, Kripa, Karṇa and others, who rescued Duryodhana from his assault. Then Dushâsana was disabled by him, Karṇa's brother slain, and Karṇa himself driven from the field by the heroic boy. At last Jayadratha, the ruler of the Sindhus, checked the rout of the Kurus, but still none could stand against Abhimanyu, Duryodhana being again beaten back on his second attempt. His son Lakshmana was slain when he assailed the young warrior, whose onset it seemed impossible to check. Then six car-warriors, Droṇa, Ashvatthâmâ, Kripa, Karṇa, Kritavarman and Vrihadvala, all rushed upon the boy together, while Jayadratha kept off all succour by charging against Yudhishṭhira. Still the youth held his own, till Droṇa bade Karṇa cut his bow to pieces with arrows, and Kritavarman slew his horses, Kripa his two charioteers; carless and bowless, he snatched up shield and sword, and when these were broken by the arrows of his well-armed foes, he caught up a car-wheel and rushed with it upraised at Droṇa. This being shivered into pieces by his assailants, he seized a mace, and driving Asvatthâmâ before him, beat down the horses and steeds of Dushâsana's son. It was his last triumph. Both combatants fell to the ground, as each levelled a blow at his antagonist, and Dushâsana's son, rising first, struck Abhimanyu on the head, and the boy "of heroic arms" went home. [§ 33-49.]

The battle ceased with Abhimanyu's fall, and great was the grief of Yudhishṭhira, who had put on him the task of penetrating into the hostile army and then had failed to support him. How should he face the bereaved Arjuna and tell him his favourite son was dead? Vyâsa came and consoled the distressed king, relating to him the origin of death, and the stories of many kings who had fallen a prey to the Goddess, and telling him that no wise man grieved for the dead; "the living man should think of the joy, the glory and the happiness of the dead." Thus saying, the holy Vyâsa disappeared and the king was comforted, but still, "with a melancholy heart he asked himself, saying, 'What shall we say unto Dhananjaya?'" [§ 50-71.]

Meanwhile that hero, returning from the field, was full of sad forebodings, and piteously appealed to Keshava for some explanation of the dread that enshrouded him. Entering the silent camp, he pressed anxiously on, till he reached his brothers sitting sad and speechless, and missed his best loved son. Then, with swift prescience, his mind grasped the truth, and he asked for Abhimanyu. "None among you, save Abhimanyu, could break that array. I, however, did not teach him how to come out of that array, after having pierced it. Did you cause the boy to enter that array?" But the father needed no answer, and he bewailed his son's death. Must he not have thought, when attacked by Droṇa and Karṇa and Kripa, "My father will in this press be my rescuer"? Could not all the Pâṇḍavas and Pânchâlas protect this boy? Did they wear armour for ornament? What were they doing when they saw Abhimanyu slain? And none dared speak to him save Shrî Krishṇa and Yudhishṭhira, who, "under all circumstances, were acceptable to Arjuna." Yudhishṭhira told him of the request to pierce the circular array, how "that child then penetrated into" it, and how, when they sought to follow and support him, Jayadratha held them in check. Then Arjuna cried: "Truly do I swear that to-morrow I will slay Jayadratha!" and he swore a fearful oath, concluding by a declaration that if the next day's sun should set without his having slain his foe, he would himself "enter the blazing fire." News of this being carried to Jayadratha, he became wild with fear and sought to leave the camp, but was persuaded to remain by promises of protection. Droṇa told him, in answer to his eager questioning, that although both he and Arjuna had received the same teaching, in consequence "of Yoga and the hard life led by Arjuna, he is superior to thee." But he himself would guard him, and form an array that Partha could not pierce. [§ *72-74*.]

Meanwhile Keshava had sternly rebuked Arjuna for making so rash a vow without seeking His counsel. In consequence of this six of the greatest Kuru warriors would be placed in front of Jayadratha, and he would be kept in the centre of an array difficult to pierce. However, He set Himself to think how Arjuna might be saved from failure on the morrow, and gave orders to prepare His own chariot and weapons in case of need. Then, as Arjuna slept, Keshava appeared to him, and drawing him from his body took him to Kailâsa, where Mahâdeva sat in splendour, and Shrî Krishṇa and Arjuna worshipped the Supreme, and obtained from Him the greatest of His weapons, the Pâshupata, for use on the morrow, and then returned rejoicing, sure of victory. [§ 75-82.]

Te fourteenth day of battle dawned, and Arjuna, leaving Yudhishṭhira in the care of Sâtyaki, sought Jayadratha in fulfilment of his vow. He had first to break his way through the elephant division, and putting this to rout he charged on Droṇa, saluting his preceptor reverently, and then assailing him, since he was the protector of Jayadratha. In vain, however, Arjuna fought against his preceptor, and at last, urged by Keshava, he evaded him and sought by making a circuit to reach his foe. Opposed by Shrutâyusha and Achyutâyusha, Arjuna was for a few moments overpowered and sank fainting against his flagstaff, but recovering, he slew his foes and again fought his way onward. At length his steeds being wounded and weary, Arjuna left his chariot and faced the rushing war chariots on foot, while Keshava bathed and refreshed the horses as though no foe were near; then, remounting, he agin faught his way onwards, though opposed by Duryodhana, encased in armour made invulnerable by Droṇa's mantras. Meanwhile Yudhishṭhira had been rendered carless by Droṇa, and was only saved from capture by the heroic Sâtyaki, who then, at Yudhishṭhira's order, followed Arjuna, and succeeded in breaking through Droṇa's division and slaying Droṇa's charioteer, so that his steeds ran away with him. Bhîma also performed prodigies of valour; he crushed the chariot of Droṇa with his mace, so that Droṇa only saved his life by leaping from it, and he drove Karṇa from the field. That warrior returning, the duel recommenced, and once, when Bhîma had Karṇa at his mercy, he refrained from slaying him, remembering Arjuna's vow; and again, when the positions were reversed, Karṇa spared Bhîma, because of his promise to Kuntî. But the sun was going down, and Arjuna's vow was still unfulfilled, while Jayadratha was hidden from his sight by his guards. Then Keshava, by Yoga, shrouded the sun, so that it seemed to be setting, and Jayadratha, thinking himself safe, exposed himself to view. And Arjuna rushed towards him and scattered his defenders, piercing his six protectors with his shafts; then he took up a terrible arrow, mantra-inspired, and shot at Jayadratha, and—warned by Keshava that the man who made Jayadratha's head fall on the ground would, by a vow of his father's, have his own head split into fragments—cutting off with this shaft his enemy's head, he sped it along with other arrows till it fell into his own father's lap, who, rising, let the head fall to the ground and himself perished under his own curse. Thus was Jayadratha slain and Arjuna's vow fulfilled, and as the sun appeared again, Arjuna drove from the field Kripa and Ashvatthâmâ, and Sâtyaki again made Karṇa carless. Nor did the battle cease at sunset, as the custom was, but continued on during the night, despite the added horrors of darkness. The chief combat of that awful night was between Ghatotkacha and Karṇa, who waged a furious duel; at last Karṇa was so hard pressed by Bhîma's Râkshasa son, and so bewildered by the illusions he created, that he caught up the invincible dart given him by Indra in exchange for his natural armour and earrings [see Vana Parva § 299-301, and 309], and levelled it at Ghatotkacha. Incapable of being baffled, the bolt struck the Râkshasa and slew him, and he fell amid the shouts of joy of the Kurus. The Pâṇḍavas, seeing him dead, began to weep, but Keshava broke into shouts of rejoicing and hugged Arjuna to His breast. Astounded at this strange outburst, Arjuna asked its reason, and Keshava told him that while Karṇa possessed that Indra-dart he could slay with it one foe, whomsoever he would; having now sped it, Arjuna's life was safe and he would be able to slay Karṇa. In truth, Karṇa was holding back that dart for the slaying of Keshava Himself, but ever forgot to use it when the opportunity came in his way. Now his power was gone, his own hope of life was shattered by his own act. Midnight had come, and the warriors, exhausted, were falling asleep, even as they fought, so Arjuna stayed the battle, until the rising of the moon. [§ 83-185.]

The battle again broke out with unabated energy, and the fifteenth day was distinguished by a fierce duel between Droṇa and Arjuna in which neither could gain any advantage. Then, avoiding each other, they attacked other foes, and the slaughter continued till Keshava suggested that some one should tell Droṇa that Ashvatthâmâ was slain. This Arjuna refused to do, but Bhîma, slaying an elephant called by that same name, called out to Droṇa, "Ashvatthâmâ hath been slain"—words true in fact but false in the sense conveyed by them. Droṇa staggered for a moment, but recovered himself, thinking the news untrue. Then many great Rishis cried to Droṇa that his hour had come for quitting the world of men, and as Dhrishṭadyumna, his destined slayer, appeared before him, his heart became cheerless. So he sent to enquire of Yudhishṭhira, who, he "firmly believed ....would never speak an untruth even for the sovereignty of the three worlds," whether his son were slain or not. Now Keshava advised Yudhishṭhira to say that Droṇa's son was dead. What! Shrî Krishṇa advised the telling of a lie? aye, thus He tested the reality of Yudhishṭhira's love of truth. Deep hidden in the nature of Yudhishṭhira there was a weakness, a disposition to rely too much on others, to shrink from taking responsibility and standing alone. Righteous, gentle, enduring, blameless in life, this weakness in his inner nature remained, and it was now to be brought to the surface and to cause his fall; he was tested and he failed. Aloud he said, "Ashvatthâmâ is dead," uttering below his breath the words "the elephant," telling a lie with his heart and seeking to maintain outer truthfulness, a subterfuge worse than a boldly spoken falsehood. As he spake, his steeds and chariot, that had been wont to remain four fingers' breadth above the ground, sank down and touched the earth—mute but eloquent testimony to his fall. Yet by that fall and the life-long sorrow of having slain his Guru by a lie, Yudhishṭhira was purged of the last weakness in his noble character, and when, at the close of life, he was again tested, when a God bade him desert his faithful dog, he rose above the trial and stood fast in righteousness, throwing away heaven that he might be faithful to the end. Thus do the Gods deal with us, trying us to the very uttermost, that any flaw may be found and gotten rid of, that in the end we may be able to stand blameless, through any stress of pain or any strain on self-reliance.

When Droṇa heard from Bhîma, on Yudhishṭhira's authority, that his son was slain, he dropped his weapons, and, sitting down on his car, gave himself to meditation. Then Dhrishṭadyumna, leaping from his chariot, seized a sword and rushed on the weaponless hero, who, bending his head, left his body, rising in radiant glory into the sky. As he rose, the lifeless body sank prone on the side of the war, and Dhrishṭadyumna, seizing the white locks, struck off the venerable head, the head of his Guru, that ancient hero of five-and-eighty years, whose disciples were the leaders of the battling hosts. In vain Arjuna cried, "Bring the preceptor alive! do not slay him! he should not be slain." Droṇa had passed ere the sword had struck him, and, glorious in the region of Brahman, was beyond all earthly pain. [§ 186-193]

At Droṇa's death, the Kuru troops broke and fled in all directions, until Ashvatthâmâ, hearing of his father's death, and inflamed to fury at the insult of seizing him by his reverend white locks, swore the death of his slayers, and summoned to his aid the mighty Nârâyaṇa weapon, capable of annihilating all foes in war. He rallied the flying forces and marshalled them again for battle. Meanwhile Arjuna, broken-hearted, was bewailing his preceptor and his own crime in being present at his cruel slaughter, though in truth he had striven to save him. "I have, O Lord!" he cried, "sunk in hell, overcome with shame." Angrily Bhîma and Dhrishṭadyumna reproached him, but Sâtyaki sided with him, bitterly rebuking Dhrishṭadyumna, until the two rushed upon each other in anger, and only the onslaught of the Kurus made them turn again upon the common foe. As Ashvatthâmâ launched his terrible weapon at the Pâṇḍava host, it blazed up consuming the troops, and Keshava shouted to them to lay down their arms and stand weaponless on the ground, so should that weapon be baffled: alone Bhîma refused to obey and stood for battle, till he was enveloped in fire, and Keshava and Arjuna dragged him down despite himself, and then the weapon vanished. Duryodhana hotly cried to Ashvatthâmâ to launch it once more, but Droṇa's son answered sadly that the weapon could not be recalled, nor used twice; Keshava had baffled it, and the destruction of the foe remained unaccomplished. Then the battle recommenced, and Bhîma's charioteer falling, he was carried away by his horses, while Arjuna attacked Asvatthâmâ, and as he issued uninjured from a shower of arrows from a celestial weapon that slew, amid the darkness it created, a whole Akshauhini of troops, Droṇa's son, heartbroken at his failure to kill Keshava and Arjuna, fled away from the field. Meeting Vyâsa, he learned from him the true nature of Keshava and Arjuna, and why his weapon could not slay them, and then he called the army to retire for the night, and the battle ceased. At its close Arjuna asked Vyâsa who was a Being he saw going before his car, and slaying those who were apparently slain by himself, and Vyâsa told him that it was Mahâdeva Himself, the Supreme Lord; he then gave him a wonderful description of the greatness of Maheshvara, and with this the Droṇa Parva closes. (§ 194-204.)

On the sixteenth day of battle, Karṇa—whose name is given to the next Parva—was made generalissimo, and the combat broke out with undiminished vigour. Karṇa fought with Nakula, depriving him of charioteer, horses and finally weapons, but spared his life for Kuntî's sake; placing his bowstring round his neck, he let him fly, vanquished and ashamed. Yudhishṭhira likewise spared Duryodhana, when the latter swooned away, wounded by the Pâṇḍava king, remembering Bhîma's vow. The day's honours again rested with Arjuna, who carried all before him; wherever the white horses flashed, guided by the divine Charioteer, victory was seen. That night Karṇa resolved to pit himself against Arjuna on the morrow, and, when the seventeenth day of battle dawned, he vowed to slay Arjuna on that day or to be himself slain by him; but he asked that Shalya, the king of the Mâdras, should be his charioteer, and thus enable him to cope with Arjuna on equal terms. At first Shalya, regarding the request as an insult, was much enraged, but Duryodhana pacified him and persuaded him to consent, since he would be pitted against Keshava Himself, and since Brahmâ Himself had once driven the chariot of Rudra. Thus Karṇa went forth to battle with Shalya as his charioteer, and the day opened inauspiciously by a quarrel between charioteer and warrior, as Shalya rebuked Karṇa for his boasting and praised Arjuna' his foe. [§ 1-45.]

Karṇa's first great combat was with Yudhishṭhira, whose car he destroyed, and who finally fled before him, but Bhîma revenged his brother's defeat, and, striking Karṇa senseless, forced his charioteer to drive him out of the battle. Soon however, returning, he engaged again in battle, and presently, meeting Yudhishṭhira with Nakula and Sahadeva, he conquered all three, and then rushed to the rescue of Duryodhana, hard pressed by Bhîma. Arjuna, meanwhile, having defeated Ashvatthâmâ, sought his elder brother, anxious as to his fate, and Yudhishṭhira welcomed him joyfully, thinking that Karṇa must be slain since Dhananjaya had left the field. On hearing, however, that Karṇa was still alive, Yudhishṭhira, smarting from his own defeat, burst out into angry reproaches against Arjuna, even taunting him with cowardice and bidding him give Gâṇḍîva to a better man. Then Arjuna drew his sword, and, on the hasty interposition of Govinda, he declared that he had vowed to slay the man who should bid him give Gâṇḍîva to another, and, slaying Yudhishṭhira, he would pay his debt to truth. Sternly Keshava reproved his friend for drawing his sword on his elder brother and king, till Arjuna submissively prayed his Lord to tell him how he might keep his vow and yet not slay the king. Then Shrî Krishṇa bade him shew some trifling disrespect to his elder brother, since disrespect killed a superior, and afterwards worship his feet and soothe him. On this Arjuna harshly addressed the king, but, heartstricken at his own disrespect, again drew his sword to slay himself in expiation of his fault. Patiently Keshava again checked him, reasoning with him till Arjuna, touching the king's feet, prayed his pardon and vowed to slay Karṇa. Then Yudhishṭhira, cut to the heart, bitterly reproached himself for his cruel words, and was fain to throw away his crown, having wronged his brother. But Govinda soothed the penitent king, and he bent down and raised the prostrate Arjuna, praising Shrî Krishṇa and lovingly embracing his brother, so that the storm was over, and Arjuna went back to the battle, blessed by Yudhishṭhịra and vowing not to return till Karṇa was slain. [§ 46-71.]

Throughout Arjuna's absence, Bhîma had been bearing the brunt of the battle, and great was his joy when the flashing diadem of Dhananjaya was again seen rushing through the press. Arjuna fought his way through till he reached Karṇa's division, staying only a brief space on the way to rescue Bhîma overborne. As Arjuna went on to reach Karṇa, Dushâsana advanced against Bhîma and a fierce duel ensued; it soon ended, however, for Bhîma hurled his terrible mace against his hated foe, and, as Dushâsana fell to the ground, he leapt to earth and, remembering Krishṇâ's wrongs and his own awful vow, he seized his sword, ripped open Dushâsana's breast, and drank some of his blood, then striking off the head of his wife's insulter. A terrible deed, that struck fear and horror into all beholders, the frightful sequel of a shameful wrong. [§ 72-83.]

And now Arjuna reached Karṇa who had just vanquished Nakula, and, slaying Karṇa's son under his father's eyes, attacked his life-long foe. The Gods themselves came to see that combat, and "the Gods were on the side of Arjuna, while the Asuras were on that of Karṇa." Fighters first with their famous bows, neither obtained any advantage, and when Arjuna invoked the Brâhma weapon, Karṇa baffled its force, and sent against his foe fierce snakes of fire. Then a mighty snake, whose mother had been slain in the burning of the forest of Khânḍava, entered Karṇa's quiver as a blazing shaft, and as, shot from Karṇa's bow, it flew through the air, Keshava pressed down Arjuna's car so that it sank a cubit's depth into the earth, while the silver steeds laid themselves flat on the ground. And the fiery snake-shaft swept off and broke into fragments the Indra-given diadem of Arjuna, but him it harmed not, as he had sunk with his chariot, thus, through Govinda, again escaping death. The snake returned to Karṇa to be again shot forth, but Karṇa refused to launch the same arrow twice, and, when the snake hurled himself at Arjuna, that warrior cut him into pieces with his shafts. Pressing his enemy hard, Arjuna made him drop his weapons, and then stayed awhile, not willing to slay his foe while he stood weaponless. But Keshava urged him on, and Karṇa, recovering, snatched up his bow, when lo! a voice said to Karṇa, "The earth is devouring thy wheel!" and the left wheel of Karṇa's car began to sink deeply into the ground. (For a Brâhmaṇa, whose calf had been heedlessly slain by Karṇa, had once cursed him, and had told him that on the approach of his death-hour, the wheel of his car should sink into the earth in battle.) [See § 42.] Then despair struck him and he began to rail at righteousness, but still fought furiously, until baffled by his sunken wheel, he sprang from his chariot to pull it up. He cried to Arjuna to wait till he had freed his wheel, praising him for his virtue and appealing to that for his protection. Then Vâsudeva said to him bitterly that he did well to remember virtue in the hour of his extremity, when he had forgotten it in all his dealings with the Pâṇḍavas, in the poisoning of Bhîma, in the house of lac, in the insults to Krishṇâ. "If the virtue that thou now invokest was nowhere on these occasions, what is the use then of parching thy palate now by uttering that word?" Then Karṇa, leaving his wheel, sped his best weapons against Arjuna, and it was Arjuna's turn to stagger back, so that Karṇa again sprang to the ground and tried to lift his wheel. Then Arjuna, recovering, shot again at his foe, cutting off his standard, and with an arrow, sped by appeal to truth and righteousness, he struck off Karṇa's head and the great warrior fell. Forth from the body of the son of the Sun-God came a radiant light, that, ascending, mingled with the Sun, and the sun-rays, nearing the setting, touching the body of Karṇa, seemed stained with his life-blood, painting the sky with crimson and then the sun itself became pallid and sank out of sight. Then the battle ceased, and the camp of the Kurus resounded with wailings as that of the Pâṇḍavas rang with joy. [§ 84-96.]

The eighteenth day opened with the election of Shalya as commander-in-chief, and the Shalya Parva tells us of his brief leadership. Yudhishṭhira led the onslaught against him and the battle raged hotly between the diminished armies. Several times the young king met his foe, and was separated from him by others, until at last, after a combat in which his driver and his steeds were slain, Yudhishṭhira discharged a blazing weapon, inspiring it with mantras, and it sheared through Shalya's chest and stretched him dead upon the ground. [§ 1-17.]

The battle still continued, though now all hope had left the Kurus save that of dying gloriously, and it raged on till of Dhritarâshṭra's sons only two—Duryodhana and Sudarsha—remained. At last, Duryodhana found himself alone, without a companion; leaving his slain steed, he fled towards a lake and took refuge in its depths, opening its water by a magic charm. Three car-warriors only had escaped slaughter, Kripa, Ashvatthâmâ and Kritavarman, on the Kuru side, and their safety was unknown to Duryodḥana, who thought himself the only survivor. Hearing from Sanjaya of the king's refuge, the three sought him after nightfall, and urged him to renew the struggle, but Duryodhana, wearied out, refused. Some hunters, approaching the lake and hearing the conversation, guessed that it was Duryodhana who had taken refuge in the lake, and went and informed the sons of Pâṇḍu, who sought out at once the hiding place of the vanquished king. Yudhishṭhira summoned him to come forth and do battle for the crown, but Duryodhana asked for a respite for a little rest, and then he would come forth and fight. Still pressed, he answered wearily that all he loved were dead; for him the earth was a desert, and he would fain retire to the woods. Let Yudhishṭhira reign over the desolated earth. Yudhishṭhira mockingly refused to take the earth as a gift from him who was now discrowned, and again challenged him to battle. "Alone, cheerless, without a car, and without an animal!" cried Duryodhana. "Alone as I am, and destitute of weapons, how can I venture to fight on foot against numerous foes all well-armed and possessed of cars." Yet the gallant spirit of the man held firm in his sore necessity. "Standing in battle, alone as I am, I shall resist all of you." And he challenged them to fight him one at a time. Yudhishṭhira consented to this wager of battle, adding that if he slew any one of them, the kingdom should be his. Then Duryodhana challenged one of the sons of Pâṇḍu to fight him on foot with the mace, and, this agreed to, he rose from the waters. Yudhishṭhira provided him with armour and with all he needed and Bhîma was put forward as his antagonist. The spectators sat round the fighters to view the struggle and Govinda's elder brother, Râma, came to see the last duel between the two warriors, that was to end their life-long rivalry. [§ 18-34.]

Râma had come thither, having set out on a pilgrimage after refusing to help either side in the war, and he had visited many tirthas, and had heard the story of Kuru tilling the field afterwards called by his name. [§ 35-54] Râma advised the combatants to return to Kurukshetra for their duel, and they according repaired thither, and the combat began. Fiercely it raged between the two mighty warriors so equally matched, each of them giving and receiving heavy blows. As they fought, Keshava reminded Arjuna of Bhîma's vow, and Arjuna struck his own left thigh in the sight of Bhîma. Bhîma took the hint, and watching his opportunity he rushed at his foe, whirling round his mace to throw it; Duryodhana leapt in the air to deceive the aim of Bhîma, and, as he leapt, Bhîma hurled his mace at the thighs of the Kuru king, fracturing them with the blow. Then Bhîma, mad with old memories of wrong, approached his helpless antagonist, and bidding him remember the insulted Draupadî, he touched his fallen head with his left foot. The kings around, seeing this, shewed signs of disapproval, and Yudhishṭhira reproved his brother: "Duryodhana is a king. He is, again, thy kinsman. He is fallen.........Do not, O Bhîma, touch a king and a kinsman with thy foot." And he pathetically recited Duryodhana's grievous losses. Then approaching his fallen enemy he comforted him, telling him that his fate was enviable thus to die, rather than to live, as must he and his brothers, under the curses of the wives of their slain kinsmen.

Râma, moreover, was furious at the foul blow struck by Bhîma, fighters with the mace not being allowed to strike below the waist, and he rushed upon Bhîma to slay him, when Keshava flung his arms round him and with gentle words soothed his anger, reminding him of Bhîma's vow. Then Râma mounted his car and went away, leaving the sons of

Pâṇḍu sad at heart. Unfairly struck down and waiting death, Duryodhana's courage did not fail him; reproached by Keshava, he answered boldly: "I have studied, made presents according to the ordinance, governed the wide earth with her seas, and stayed over the heads of my foes. Who is there so fortunate as myself? That end again which is coveted by Kshattriyas observant of the duties of their own order, death in battle, hath become mine; who, therefore, is so fortunate as myself? Human enjoyments such as were worthy of the very Gods, and such as could with difficultly be obtained by other kings, have been mine. Prosperity of the very highest kind has been attained by me. Who then is so fortunate as myself? With all my well-wishers and my younger brothers I am going to heaven, O Thou of unfading glory! As regards yourselves, with your purposes unachieved and torn by grief, live ye in this unhappy world." It was a hero-heart that in the hour of defeat, in bodily agony, and surrounded by triumphant foes, could thus rejoice exultantly: obstinate, cruel, unscrupulous, had Duryodhana been, but he was strong and brave. [§ 55-61.]

As the Pâṇḍavas reached their quarters, Keshava bade Arjuna remove Gâṇḍîva and his quivers from his car and descend in front of Him. Then Keshava

Himself left the chariot and the ape on the banner disappeared, and lo! in a moment, car, reins, steeds, yoke and shaft fell into ashes. Amazed, Arjuna enquired the reason of this strange event, and Govinda replied: "That car, O Arjuna, had before been consumed by diverse kinds of weapons. It was because I had sat on it during battle that it did not fall into pieces, O scorcher of foes! Previously consumed by the energy of Brâhma weapons it has been reduced to ashes on My abandoning it after attainment by thee of thy objects." Truly had Keshava shewed Himself throughout that deadly battle the Friend and Protector of Arjuna, and proven once again that "where Krishṇa is, there is victory."

Then Yudhishṭhira prayed Keshava to go to Hastinâpura, and break to Gândhârî the news of her son's death. Would not the wrath of that pure ascetic blaze up and consume her son's enemies, unless Shrî Krishṇa Himself bore to her the fatal news? So the Lord went forth, and, reaching Hastinâpura, gently saluted the bereaved parents, weeping as he grasped the blind king's hand. Gravely and softly He reminded them of the events that had forced the Pâṇḍavas into the war that had ended so fatally for their oppressors. He appealed to Gândhârî, reminding her of her own words to her son, and she conquered her grief enough to speak: "It is even so, O Keshava, as Thou sayest. My heart, burning in grief, had been unsteadied. After hearing Thy words, however, that heart, O Janârdana, hath again become steady. As regards the blind old king, now become childless, thou, O foremost of men, with those heroes, the sons of Pâṇḍu, hast become his refuge." Thus saying, she covered her face and burst again into tears. Then Keshava knew that Droṇa's son was meditating evil against the Pâṇḍavas, and rising hastily, He took leave, explaining that Ashvatthâmâ was plotting to destroy the Pâṇḍavas that night. Then the blind king and his wife bade Him go swiftly and protect the sons of Pâṇḍu, and He drove back to the camp and went to those He loved. [§ 62, 63.]

Meanwhile Duryodhana lay dying, and was found stretched on the ground by Kripa Asvatthâmâ and Kritavarman, who sorely bewailed his fall. Then Asvatthâmâ prayed the dying king to give him permission to slay the conquerors, and Duryodhana bade Kripa instal Droṇa's son as general. General, truly, without an army, but still not a foe to be despised, as the sequel proved. And with this ceremony the Shalya Parva ends. [§ 64, 65.]

The brief Sauptika Parva gives the story of the vengeance taken by Ashvatthâmâ for his father's death. He decided to attack the sleeping host of the sons of Pâṇḍu, and, despite the efforts of Kripa to dissuade him, he went to the entrance of their camp. He was foiled by a mighty Being who stood there, into whose body his weapons penetrated without effect, and then, worshipping Rudra, and entering into the sacrificial fire, offering up himself as victim, he obtained from Mahâdeva the power to accomplish his object. Entering the camp at dead of night, he slaughtered his sleeping enemies, Dhrishṭadyumna first of all, with the sons of Draupadî, till none were left alive, save the five sons of Pâṇḍu and Sâtyaki and Keshava Himself, who were not there. Returning to the dying Duryodhana, with Kripa and Kritavarman, he told him of the destruction of his foes. It brought a last gleam of satisfaction to the agonising king, and with the words: "Good be to you all. Prosperity be yours. All of us will again meet in heaven," he quietly breathed his last [§ 1-9.]

Yudhishṭhira, on hearing the grievous news, sent for Draupadî, who, broken-hearted, took a vow to die if Ashvatthâmâ were not slain, and the gem on his head, born with him, brought to her. Bhîma setting forth to pursue Ashvatthâmâ, Keshava desired Yudhishṭhira and Arjuna to come with Him on His car, as Bhîma could not cope with the celestial weapon Brahmashira, known to Droṇa's son, and they overtook Bhîma as he was just reaching Ashvatthâmâ. The latter taking up a blade of grass, turned it by mantras into the great celestial weapon, while Arjuna quickly obeying Keshava, hurled against Ashvatthâmâ the same celestial weapon, the use of which he had learned from Droṇa himself. Then Nârada and Vyâsa threw themselves between these weapons and held them in check, and Arjuna, "submissive and obedient to all his superiors," withdrew his weapon in reverence, a feat that none save the chaste in heart might do. Ashvatthâmâ, however, was unable to withdraw his, but desirous of shewing reverence to the Rishis, he turned it to slay only the unborn children of the Pâṇḍava women, and gave the gem born with him from his head. Despite his slaughter of the children, Keshava declared that one of them should live, revived by Himself, and should rule over the kingdom of the Pâṇḍavas as Parikshit, while Ashvatthâmâ himself should, for his wicked act, roam lonely over the earth for three thousand years, "without a companion and without being able to talk with any one." Keshava returned with Nârada and the princes to Draupadî, who, receiving the gem and hearing that Ashvatthâmâ was deprived of his weapons and left to roam the earth, forgave him as the son of the preceptor, Droṇa, and gave up her vow. Then Krishṇa explained that Ashvatthâmâ had slain the survivors in the battle by the will of Mahâdeva. [§ 10-11.]

Meanwhile king Dhritarâshṭra, mourning for his sons and his people, called all the women of the royal household to follow him to the obsequies of the slain, and they set out from Hastinâpura, a mournful procession, fulfilling the prophecy spoken to Krishṇâ when she was driven forth in tears. On their way they met Ashvatthâmâ, Kripa and Kritavarman returning from the slaughter of the Pânḍava host, the three parting after leaving the king, and Ashvatthâmâ going on alone, to encounter the princes, as we have seen. Yudhishṭhira, with his brothers, Keshava and Krishṇâ, hearing of Dhritarâshṭra's coming, went forth to meet the king, who gently embraced Yudhishṭhira. But when Bhîma was approaching, the blind king's wrath blazed up, and he was going to strangle Bhîma as he flung his arms round him, when the ever-watchful Keshava thrust into Bhîma's place an iron image, which was crushed by the grip of Dhritarâshṭra, who sank bleeding to the ground, his own chest bruised by the strong embrace. Then remorse struck the king and he cried aloud, "Alas! O Bhîma!" till Keshava, seeing his wrath was spent, explained what He had done and that no harm had been wrought. The king, confessing his own faults, and saying that he had fallen away from righteousness from parental affection, then embraced the sons of Pâṇḍu and blessed them, accepting them as his own. Gândhârî also pardoned them, after a struggle with her anger, burning with the fierce fire that her ascetic life had given her, a fire so effective to consume her enemies that when she directed her downward glance from within the folds that covered her eyes on the foot of Yudhishṭhira, the spot where that glance fell was scorched as by a physical flame.*

Now Gândhârî was endowed with a high form of what is now called clairvoyance, or astral vision, and she "saw from a distance, but as if from a near point, that field of battle where the Kuru hosts lay slaughtered." Piteously she described scene after scene to Keshava, until she reached the burning of the bodies of her sons, and then, overcome by grief, she lifted up her voice against Shrî Krishna: "By the little

* It is interesting to know that this force of the will, which read of here, may be mocked as a "superstition," has been proved by modern science to exist, and burns have been made by "hypnotic suggestion."

merit I have acquired through waiting dutifully on my husband, by that merit so difficult to obtain, I shall curse Thee, O wielder of the discus and the mace! Since Thou wert indifferent to the Kurus and the Pâṇḍavas whilst they slew each other, therefore, O Govinda, Thou shalt be the slayer of Thine own kinsmen. On the thirtysixth year from this, O slayer of Madhu, Thou shalt, after causing the slaughter of Thy kinsmen and friends and sons, perish by shameful means within the wilderness." The mighty Lord of life and death, knowing all things beforehand, answered with a faint sad smile: "There is none in the world save Myself that is capable of exterminating the Vrishnis. I know it well. I am endeavouring to bring it about. In denouncing this curse, O thou of excellent vows, thou hast aided Me in the accomplishment of that task." So surely do our wildest follies but work towards the fulfilment of the divine purposes.

On Gangâ's banks a vast concourse of mourners gathered to offer oblations to the slain warriors, and there Kuntî, broken down with grief, revealed to the sons of Pâṇḍu that Karṇa had been born of her, the child of the Sun-God, and that he was thus their elder brother. Then the five brothers burst into loud lamentations, and Yudhishṭhira bewailed the dead hero, crying that if this had been known the whole terrible carnage might have been prevented. [Strî Parva, § 1-27.]

The young king, his brothers, and the mourners, remained awhile on the banks of Gangâ, and thither came Nârada and other Rishis, to whom Yudhishṭhira poured out his bitter grief for Karṇa, for having slain unwittingly his elder brother. Why, he asked in conclusion, had the earth swallowed up Karṇa's wheel? what curse was on him? Nârada then related to the princes the story of Karṇa, and told how, on being refused by Droṇa the knowledge of the Brâhma weapon, since he was neither a Brâhmaṇa nor an ascetic Kshattriya, he had gone to Râma and to him had falsely represented himself to be a Brâhmaṇa of Bhrigu's race, and had become his pupil. While with him he had been cursed by a Brâhmaṇa, for the heedless slaying of his cow, to be beheaded by his foe when the earth swallowed his chariot wheel in battle. Moreover Râma, discovering by his extraordinary endurance of pain that he was not a Brâhmaṇa, cursed him for his falsehood, declaring that he should forget the Brâhma weapon in the hour of his need. Yudhishṭhira could not be comforted, however, for the slaying of his elder brother, and passionately declared that, resigning the kingdom to Arjuna, he would betake himself to an ascetic life. A long discussion followed, his brothers, Krishṇâ and various Rishis remonstrating with the heartbroken prince, until at last he yielded to their entreaties, and consented to wear the crown. Then he set forth for Hastinâpura, following king Dhritarâshṭra, who rode in the place of honour, and amid the chorus of welcomes only one discordant note was heard. A Râkshasa friend of Duryodhana, named Chârvâka, disguised himself as a Brâhmaṇa, and cried fie! on the king for having slain his kinsmen, assuming to speak in the name of the Brâhmaṇas present. Yudhishṭhira answered meekly, thinking the Brâhmaṇas were angry with him, offering to lay down his life. But the Brâhmaṇas cried out blessings on him, repudiating Chârvâka, who fell dead as they uttered "Hun!"—the sound slaying the offender. Then was Yudhishṭhira installed as king amid the joyous acclamations of the people, and the young king, declaring himself to be only the servant of Dhritarâshṭra, appointed officers to the kingdom to rule it righteously, caused the Shrâddha rites to be duly performed, erected houses for giving food and water, and excavated tanks in the names of the dead, provided tenderly for the widows and mothers of the slain, gave alms to the poor, and then, praising Shrî Krishṇa in a noble hymn, he bade his brothers rest, and the earth too had peace. [Shânti Parva, § 1-46]

—:o:—

CHAPTER VIII.

THE ÇREAT EXHORTATION.

We have left our greatest hero lying on the field of battle on his bed of anguish, and there in truth he lay through all the events we have glanced at, till the fighting was over and king Yudhishṭhira was installed as monarch. But now the last scenes are approaching, and the greater part of the Shânti Parva the longest Parva in the "Mahâbhârata," as well as the whole Anushâshana Parva, is devoted to these closing scenes, and to the wonderful exposition of Dharma given by the dying hero.

Yudhishṭhira, going to see Shrî Krishṇa, found Him seated in meditation, robed in yellow and blazing with gems; "so beautiful did He look that simile there is none in the three worlds." He answered naught to the king's questions, being wholly abstracted, and Yudhishṭhira, worshipping Him, asked wonderingly why He, the mighty God, should practise yoga. Then Keshava answered, smiling, that Bhîshma "is thinking of me. Hence is My mind also concentrated on him." What a light shines out from these gentle words. When a worshipper has fixed his thoughts on God, God thinks of him, the turning of the heart to God draws His attention. Shrî Krishṇa went on to advise Yudhishṭhira to go and learn from Bhîshma ere he passed away whatever he needed to know as to duty; "when Bhîshma, that foremost one of Kuru's race, disappears from earth, every kind of knowledge will disappear with him." Yudhishṭhira assenting, and praying Govinda to bless the dying warrior with His presence, Shrî Krishṇa's car was yoked, and they set forth for Kurukshetra with an illustrious train. On the field meanwhile Bhishma was lying, thinking "of Krishṇa in mind, word and act," uttering to Him a noble hymn that you should all study. He adored Keshava in form after form, seeing Him in all and all in Him, till his love drew loving response and the Holy One came to His devotee.

Approaching "Bhîshma stretched on his arrowy bed, and resembling in splendour the evening sun covered with his own rays," Vâsudeva spoke to him tenderly and begged him to instruct Yudhishṭhira as to duty, thus dispelling the grief he felt for the slaying of his kinsmen. Bhîshma answered with loving devotion, praying the Lord to bless him, and Vâsudeva replied that he had yet six and fifty days to live, and that when he went "all knowledge, O hero, will expire with thee. It is for this that all these persons assembled together have approached thee, to listen to words on duty and morality. Do thou then speak words of truth, fraught with morality and profit and yoga." But Bhîshma asked: "What words, O Master of speech, can I say in Thy presence?" And he pleaded in excuse the anguish of his wounds, the clouding of his mind and his failing strength. "I am only barely alive. Do Thou, therefore, Thyself speak for the good of king Yudhishṭhira the just, for Thou art the ordainer of all the ordinances. How, O Krishṇa, when Thou, the eternal Creator of the universe, art present, can one like me speak, like a disciple in the presence of the Guru?" Then Keshava blessed him, relieving him of his agony; "Discomfort and stupefaction and burning and pain and hunger and thirst, O son of Gangâ, shall not overcome thee, O thou of unfading glory. Thy perceptions and memory shall be unclouded, O sinless one. Thy understanding shall not fail thee." With this, Keshava went away, for the sun was setting, and music sounded softly as flowers fell from heaven and fragrant breezes blew. [§ 46-52.]

The five sons of Pâṇḍu accompanied Vâsudeva to Bhîshma in the morning, and thither also came the surviving kings and many Rishis, headed by

Nârada. In reply to Govinda's gentle question, Bhîshma said gratefully that all suffering had left him by the Lord's grace, and all knowledge had come to him by that same favour. But why should not He, the Giver, Himself speak as Teacher? With exquisite tenderness the Lord answered that nothing could add to His glory who was the root of fame and all good things, but He willed that the fame of His devotee should spread over the world and that he might live by that fame as long as earth should last. As a father to his sons let Bhîshma teach of Dharma, for he had never transgressed duty and was therefore competent to teach. Then Bhîshma answered: "I shall discourse on Dharma. My speech and mind have become steady through Thy grace, O Govinda, who art the eternal Soul of every being." And he bade Yudhishṭhira question him, since he was a fit pupil; in him were intelligence, self-restraint, chastity, forgiveness, righteousness, mental vigour and energy, and he was therefore fit to learn. For the disciple must be worthy as well as the Guru, the pupil as well as the teacher, else is teaching useless; if the pupil do not practise morality, how may the subtle lessons of duty be profitably given? But Yudhishṭhira feared to approach, said Shrî Krishṇa, having pierced those who deserved his worship. Calmly spoke the noble Bhîshma, just and dutiful, despite all the agony he had undergone, declaring that it was the duty of the Kshattriya to slay in battle even his Guru, if he engaged in an unjust battle with him. And as Yudhishṭhira in passionate grief and gratitude seized his feet, the hero welcomed him, and bade him sit: "Do not fear, O best of the Kurus. Ask me, O child, without any anxiety." [§ 53-55.]

First, Yudhishṭhira would know of kingly duties, and on this theme Bhîshma spoke at length, giving us the old ideal of kingship, of royalty as it should be, the minister of the Gods on earth. In the first place the king must be religious, a worshipper of Gods and Brâhmaṇas, and next he should show promptitude and exertion. In failure he should redouble his efforts; "this is the high duty of kings." He must be devoted to truth and administer justice, being neither too indulgent nor too severe. He must love his people, as the mother the child of her womb, seeking their good as the mother the good of the child. To benefit his people he must sacrifice his own pleasure, and never lose fortitude, being ever ready in action. "The happiness of their subjects, observance of truth, and sincerity of behaviour, are the eternal duty of kings." He should be dignified, self-controlled, affable, deferential to the aged, splendid and liberal. His subjects should live in his kingdom like sons in the house of their father. "He is, indeed, a king whose subjects are engaged in their respective duties, and do not fear to cast off their bodies when duty bids; whose people, duly protected, are all of peaceful behaviour, obedient, docile, tractable, unwilling to engage in disputes and inclined to liberality." To protect his subjects is the cream of kingly duties. "The hero who acts is superior to the hero who talks."

But why should one man rule, asked Yudhishṭhira. At first, answered Bhîshma, there was no king, all men righteously protecting one another, but as men became covetous, kingship became necessary for protection, and the Gods gave celestial men to be the rulers; later, men of great merit were reborn on earth as kings, and obedience was gladly rendered to one seen to be superior. Hence was it said that there was no difference between a God and a King. [§ 55-59.] After explaining the four orders and the four modes of life, Bhîshma pointed out that all these had their root and place in kingly duties, and the king was the protector of all. [§ 60-66.] Anarchy was the worst possible state, and no one should dwell in kingdoms torn by anarchy. Suffering under the oppression of the strong, men had prayed for a king, and Manu was sent to regulate respective duties and check evil acts. [§ 67.] After dilating further on royal duties in detail [§ 68-74], Bhîshma pointed out that the king incurred the sin—the karmic responsibility—for any distress or evil in his kingdom arising from his neglect of his duty of protecting his subjects. Once a king was seized by a Râkshasa, but he urged that in his realm were no thieves, nor criminals, nor drinkers of alcohol, nor irreligious persons, while the four castes all did their respective duties. He had supported the helpless and the old, the weak, the sick, and forlorn women. He had fought for his people and for justice, and his people ever blessed him. What then could a Râkshasa do to him? Then the Râkshasa let him go. [§ 75-77.] After a digression treating of the way in which irregularities should be dealt with [§ 78-90], Bhîshma uttered a solemn warning as to the danger of trampling on the weak. "The Creator created Power (represented by the king), for the sake of protecting weakness.........The eyes of the weak, of the muni, and of the snake of virulent poison, should be regarded as unbearable. Do not therefore come into hostile contact with the weak. Thou shouldst regard the weak as being always subject to humiliation. Take care that the eyes of the weak do not burn thee with thy kinsmen. In a race scorched by the eyes of the weak, no children take birth. Such eyes burn the race to its very roots. Do not therefore come into (hostile) contact with the weak! Weakness is more powerful than even the greatest power, for that power which is scorched by weakness becomes totally exterminated. If a person who has been humiliated or struck, fail, while shrieking for assistance, to obtain a protector, divine chastisement overtakes the king and brings about his destruction. Do not, O Sire, while in enjoyment of power, take wealth from those that are weak. Take care that the eyes of the weak do not burn thee like a blazing fire. The tears shed by weeping men afflicted by falsehoods slay the children and animals of those that have uttered those falsehoods.........When a weak person fails to find a rescuer, the great rod of divine chastisement falls (upon the king). [§ 91.]

Bhîshma then turns to the duties of warriors, pointing out that men should fight without anger and bloodthirstiness, should never take an unfair advantage, nor strike a disabled foe. The wounded should be sent home, or nursed, and even the wicked should be subdued by fair means. Better to lose life than to gain victory unrighteously. Thus men were trained in Kshattriya duties, learning useful lessons in war itself. [§ 95.]

While this earlier part of the Great Exhortation deals with duties belonging to royalty and warfare, many of the precepts given are useful to all of us. Thus when Bhîshma urges on the king the necessity for promptitude and exertion he remarks that he regards exertion as superior to destiny, for destiny is the result of previous exertion. [§ 56.] Nowadays, we sometimes hear people say that exertion is useless, since all is destiny, or karma. Bhîshma never falls into that mistake, for he understands the workings of karma, and knows that it does not deprive exertion of its value. The karma that we reap now is the result of our past exertion, and present exertion can modify this karma. We are not straws in the current of karma, but men, nay, Gods in the making. Our mental powers, feelings, desires, passions are indeed our karma, but we created them by our exertions, and we have not lost that power of exertion which can modify in the present what it created in the past. So again the king is told not to abandon fortitude. [§ 56.] This, too, is for all. A man should be strong, able to endure. The tendency of modern civilisation is to make everything smooth and easy, to give the body all it asks, and to shrink from hardships. Learn to be strong. Do not mind so much being uncomfortable. Train your bodies to endurance.

Our bodies should be our slaves, not our masters. There is too much physical softness in modern life, and such softness weakens. Or take again the story of the king seized by the Râkshasa [§ 77]. The king was fearless, because he had done his duty. The man who does his duty need never fear. Harm can only touch us when duty has been forgotten or neglected. Nothing can do us hurt, no circumstances can injure us, no power can break us down, while we do right. We are timid and troubled because we are conscious of wrong thinking and wrong doing, and these open our gates to the enemy and we fear his assaults. Shut the gates, and no foe can enter. Bhîshma shews his greatness as teacher by his keen insight into the difference between appearance and reality; thus he says: "There is a declaration in the Vedas that penances are higher than sacrifices. I shall now speak to thee of penances. O learned prince, listen to me. Abstention from injury, truthfulness of speech, benevolence, compassion—these are regarded as penances by the wise, and not the emaciation of the body." [§ 79.] The same idea comes out in the story of king Janaka and Sulabhâ, a female ascetic. The king argued that the wearing of brown cloths, shaving of the head, bearing of the triple stick and kamandula—these are the outward signs of one's mode of life. These have no value in aiding one to attain emancipation.......I am living in a condition of freedom, though ostensibly engaged in the enjoyment of religion, wealth, pleasure, in the form of kingdom and spouses, which constitute a field of bondage (for most). The bonds constituted by kingdom and wealth, and the bondage of attachments, I have cut off with the sword of renunciation." [§ 321.]. A man may renounce outwardly or inwardly, and the latter is the harder of the two. A Yogî is not a Yogî by his brown cloth, but by his steady mind and broken bonds of desire. A man may be a yogî in any dress and without any outer signs of ascetic life. Surrounded by objects he may be without attachments, holding wealth he may not be held by it, surrounded by possessions he may be without the feeling "these are mine." Those only are honoured by the Gods and the wise who are yogîs in heart and in the inner life; they are the true sannyâsîs. Boys and young men in whom the spiritual life is dawning often feel a passionate desire to run away from the world to the jungle, to escape from the drudgery of worldly duties into the calm of the outwardly ascetic life. For the most part the path of duty does not lie that way. The spiritual life may be led in the world, though the road be a hard one. To live in the world indifferent to its attractions, to be outwardly a man of the world and inwardly an ascetic, that is the demand made on many to-day. And in this there is no greater teacher than Bhîshma, the ruler, the statesman, the warrior, and yet the yogî of steady mind, of controlled passions, blameless from birth to death.

In his review of human duties Bhîshma now takes up those of general obligation. And he puts in the forefront a duty which in modern days is falling out of sight with very many: "The worship of father, mother and guru is most important according to me." If that be neglected, nothing else is well done. Reverence, veneration, submission, humility these lie at the root of character. "The father is superior to ten Upâdhyayas. The mother, again, is superior to ten fathers, or perhaps to the whole world in importance. There is no one that deserves such reverence as the mother. In my opinion, however, the guru is worthy of greater reverence than the father or even the mother. The father and the mother are authors of one's being. The life, on the other hand, obtained from one's guru is heavenly. That life is subject to no decay and is immortal." In modern India, reverence for parents is still found far more than in any other land, though even this is being undermined by the subtle workings of the false western idea of "independence." But the old sweet and sacred tie between Guru and shishya has well-nigh disappeared; and, as ever, it is the superior who is to blame. The failure of the Guru in the two great duties he owes to his shishya, love and guidance, has led to the failure of the shishya in his duties, reverence and trust. "Gurus always shew great affection for their disciples," said Bhîshma, speaking of the facts of his time. "The latter should therefore shew their gurus commensurate reverence." Yet even in these modern days Gurus may yet be found who, faithfully performing their duties, enable the disciple to perform his; the great responsibility ever lies with the superior, and the rare appearance of a true Guru has led to the equally rare appearance of true disciples. [§ 108.]

The great teacher then answered a variety of questions put by Yudhishṭhira, from which we can only select a few. The young king enquired as to the nature of Dharma, and Bhîshma, after explaining the difficulty of defining it, gave some rules by which it might be partly known. "Dharma was ordained for the advancement and growth of all creatures. Therefore that which leads to advancement and growth is Dharma. Dharma was ordained for restraining creatures from injuring one another. Therefore that is Dharma which prevents injury to creatures. Dharma is so called because it upholds all creatures. In fact all creatures are upheld by Dharma. Therefore that is Dharma which is capable of upholding all creatures." [§ 109.] How might a man overcome difficulties? "They that never practise deceit, they whose behaviour is restrained by salutary restrictions, and they that control all worldly desires, succeed in overcoming all difficulties. They that do not speak when addressed in evil language, they that do not injure others when injured themselves, they that give but do not take, succeed in overcoming all difficulties......They that do not commit any kind of sin in thought, word, and deed, they that never injure any creature, succeed in overcoming all difficulties...... They that always speak the truth in this world, even when life is at stake, and that are examples for all creatures to imitate, succeed in overcoming all difficulties. They whose acts never deceive, whose words are always agreeable, and whose wealth is always well spent, succeed in overcoming all difficulties...... They that bow to all the Gods, that listen to the doctrines of all creeds, that have faith, and are endued with tranquil souls, succeed in overcoming all difficulties." [§ 110.] How should a wise man bear abuse? asked the young king. "An intelligent man," answered Bhîshma, "should disregard an utterer of abusive language, who resembles, after all, only a Tittibha uttering dissonant cries.........The man of wisdom should endure everything that such a person of limited intelligence may say. What can a vulgar man do by either his praise or blame? He is even like a crow that caws uselessly in the woods." [§ 114.] Many people make their lives very uneasy by continually fretting over what others may think or say of them; try and do the right, seeking neither praise nor blame, but learning from both how to do better. A man's life should be regulated, not running into extremes. Men seek virtue, wealth and pleasure; "wealth has its root in virtue, and pleasure is said to be the fruit of wealth." In seeking wealth man must not disregard virtue, nor seek pleasure at the cost of virtue and wealth. "The dross of virtue consists in the desire for reward; the dross of wealth consists in hoarding it; when purged of these impurities, they are productive of great results." [§ 123.] Very nobly did Bhîshma speak of truth. "Truth is an eternal duty. One should reverentially bow to truth. Truth is the highest refuge. Truth is duty; truth is penance; truth is yoga; truth is the eternal Brahman. Truth hath been said to be sacrifice of a high order. Everything rests on truth......The forms that truth assumes are impartiality, self-control, forgiveness, modesty, endurance, goodness, renunciation, contemplation, dignity, fortitude, compassion and abstention from injury." He then explains how these are forms of truth, and concludes: "There is no duty which is higher than truth, and no sin more heinous than untruth. Indeed, truth is the very foundation of righteousness.........Once on a time a thousand horse-sacrifices and truth were weighed against each other in the balance. Truth weighed heavier than a thousand horse-sacrifices." [§ 162.] Every Indian boy should study this section and live it. Lying degrades the whole character. To do a deceitful thing lowers a boy, makes him mean and contemptible. The boy who lies or cheats is no true Hindu, no true Aryan.

Now men in this world suffer much, and the roots of suffering lie in their ignorance. They covet external things, whereas happiness consists in realising inner things, in knowing that "dear Self in whom there is nothing but tranquillity......that dear Supreme Self, and in casting off all desire for worldly objects." [§ 174.] Poverty, which men so much dread, only takes away external things and really relieves us from many sources of anxiety and trouble. If a man has found peace in the Self, and desires nothing, then "complete poverty, in this world, is happiness. It is a good regimen, it is the source of blessings, it is freedom from danger. This foeless path is unattainable (by persons cherishing desire) and is easily attained (by those that are freed from desire). Casting my eyes on every part of the three worlds, I do not behold the person who is equal to a poor man of pure conduct and without attachment (to worldly things). I weighed poverty and sovereignty in a balance. Poverty weighed heavier than sovereignty and seemed to possess greater merits." [§ 175.] But thus to feel implies that desires have been gotten rid of, and on this is recited the song that Manki sung when freed from his long bondage to desire. Greedy of wealth, Manki searched for it long, but ever was he doomed to disappointment. With the last remnant of his property he bought a pair of calves to train up for the plough. But evil fate ordained that the cord with which the two were tied should get entangled with a passing camel, so that both were killed. This last mischance opened the heart of Manki, so that desire fled thence unconfined, and Manki burst forth into song: "He that desires happiness must renounce Desire. Well Shuka said that of these two, the one who gets all that he wishes, and the one who casts off every wish, the latter, who renounces all, is surely much superior to the former, for none can ever attain to the end of all desires. Do thou, O my soul! so long a slave to greed, taste now for once the joys of freedom and tranquillity. Long have I slept, but I shall sleep no longer: I shall wake. No more shalt thou deceive me, O Desire! Whatever object thou settest heart upon, thou didst force me to follow it, heedless and never pausing to enquire if it was easy or impossible to gain. Thou art without intelligence. Thou art a fool. Ever unsatisfied, thou burnest like a fire, always lambent for more offering. Thou art impossible to fill, like space itself. Thy one wish is to plunge me into sorrow. This day we part; from this day, O Desire! I can no more live in thy company. I think no more of thee and of thy train. I cast thee off with all the passions of my heart. I who was harassed with despair before, have now attained to perfect peace of mind. In full contentment of the heart, senses at ease, shall I live henceforth on what I can get, and labour not again for satisfaction of thy wishes, O my foe. Casting thee off and all thy train, I gain at once instead tranquillity and self-restraint, forgiveness and compassion and deliverance." Thus Manki lost a little, and gained all. [Summarised from § 177.]

Freedom from desire is gained by knowledge, and to this end meditation, or the practice of yoga, is recommended. Difficult as it is, it must be followed, and Bhîshma gives some directions that are as helpful now as they were when they were spoken five thousand years ago. Living in a place "favorable to perfect tranquillity of heart," the Yogî sits, subduing all the senses, and with mind one-pointed towards the Supreme Soul, in meditation. "He has no perception of sound through the ear; no perception of touch through the skin; no perception of form through the eye; no perception of taste through the tongue; nor has he any perception of scent through the organ of smell. Immersed in yoga, rapt in meditation, he abandons all things." With mind alert and energetic, he gives up all "desire for anything that excites the five senses." Thus "withdrawing his five senses into the mind, he should then fix the unstable mind with the five senses (in the Intellect). Patiently should the Yogî fix his mind, which always wanders, so that his five gates [his five senses] may be made stable in respect of things that are themselves unstable. He should, in the firmament of the heart, fix his mind in the path of meditation, making it independent of the body or any other refuge." "I have spoken of the path of meditation first, since the Yogî has first to control his senses and his mind (and direct them to that path). The mind which constitutes the sixth (sense), when thus restrained, seeks to flash out like the capricious and flighty lightning moving in frolic among the clouds. As a drop of water on a (lotus) leaf is unstable and moves about in all directions, even so becomes the Yogî's mind when first fixed in the path of meditation. When fixed, for a while the mind stays in that path; when, however, it strays again into the path of the wind, it becomes as flighty as the wind. The person conversant with the ways of yoga-meditation, undiscouraged by this, never regarding the loss of the toil undergone, casting aside idleness and malice, should again direct his mind to meditation. When one, observing the vow of silence, begins to set his mind on yoga, then discrimination, knowledge, and power to avoid evil, are gained by him. Though feeling annoyed in consequence of the flightiness of his mind, he should fix it (in meditation, again and again). Never should the Yogî despair." [§ 195.] Only by perseverance can success be gained, but the gaining of success is certain by perseverance; and then comes the joy which can never otherwise be reached, higher than anything else on earth, the joy of union with the one Self, supreme tranquillity, perfect peace. "By casting off, with the aid of yoga, these five faults, attachment, heedlessness, affection, lust and wrath, one attains to emancipation." [§ 301.] Truly the road of yoga is no easy one. In fact, "This high path of learned Brâhmaṇas is exceedingly difficult to tread. No one can walk along this path with ease. That path is like a terrible forest which abounds with innumerable snakes and crawling vermin, with (concealed) pits occurring everywhere, without water for slaking one's thirst, and full of thorns, and inaccessible on that account. Indeed, the path of yoga is like a road along which no edibles occur, which runs through a desert having all its trees burnt down in a conflagration, and which has been rendered unsafe by being infested with bands of robbers. Very few young men can pass safely through it. Like unto a path of this nature, few Brâhmaṇas can tread the yoga path with ease and comfort. That man who having betaken himself to this path ceases to go forward (but turns back after having made some progress), is regarded as guilty of many faults. Men of cleansed souls, O Lord of earth! can stay with ease upon yoga-contemplation, which is like the sharp edge of a razor. Persons of uncleansed souls, however, cannot stay on it. [§ 301.]

Further, Bhîshma instructs the young king on many deep philosophic truths, such as karma, nature, man, and that which may be known of God. Here is matter for long and patient study, and we can only glance briefly at a few of the teachings, that we may see how vast is the reach of this great epic, how profound and luminous its expositions. Karma is a relation between actions, that which makes one grow out of another, linking all into a chain of causes and effects, and thus binding the actor. It exists in and through desire, desire being the adhesive quality in nature. By our desires we attach ourselves to objects, and we are born again and again in the places where the objects are found to which we have thus attached ourselves. "Whatever acts are accomplished by means of the body, one enjoys the fruits thereof in a state of physical existence.........Whatever acts are accomplished by means of words, their fruits are to be enjoyed in a state in which words can be spoken. So whatever acts are accomplished by the mind, their fruits are enjoyed in a state in which one is not freed from the mind. Devoted to the fruits of acts, whatever kind of acts a person covetous of fruits accomplishes, the fruits, good or bad, that he actually enjoys partake of their character. Like fishes going against a current of water, the acts of a past life are flung back on the actor. The embodied creature experiences happiness for his good acts, and misery for his evil ones." [§ 201.] "As vessels of white brass, when steeped in liquified gold or silver, catch the hue of these metals, even so a living creature, who is completely dependent on the acts of his past lives, takes his colour from the character of those acts. Nothing can sprout forth without a seed. No one can obtain happiness without having accomplished acts capable of leading to happiness......As the fruit of his acts, O king, a person sometimes obtains happiness only, sometimes misery in the same way, and sometimes happiness and misery blended together. Whether righteous or sinful, acts are never destroyed (except by experiencing their fruits). Sometimes, O child, the happiness due to good acts remains concealed and covered in such a way that it does not display itself, in the case of the person who is sinking in life's ocean, till his sorrows disappear. After sorrow has been exhausted, enjoyment begins. And know, O king, that upon the exhaustion of the fruit of good acts, those of sinful acts begin to manifest themselves. Self-restraint, forgiveness, patience, energy, contentment, truthfulness of speech, modesty, abstention from injury, freedom from vicious practices, and cleverness—these are productive of happiness. No creature is eternally subject to the fruits of his good or bad acts.........One never has to enjoy or endure the good and bad acts of another. Truly, one enjoys and endures the fruits of those acts only that one does oneself." [§ 291.]

In a conversation between Manu and Vrihaspati, recounted by Bhîshma, are given the outlines (details are omitted) of some of the fundamental conceptions of Hinduism regarding the one Existence and the many. From "the eternal and undeteriorating One" came forth in the aspect of matter the five great Elements in due succession; their root is the "One without a second," and this One, who "does all things is the cause. Everything else is effect." This is the the SELF, Unmanifested. From This, in the aspect of consciousness, springs the manifested Self in man identical in nature with the Unmanifested; from this the Understanding is evolved, and from the Understanding the Mind; to the Mind the Senses are added, and these five make up the Dweller in the Body, which Body is formed of the five Elements. As the sun sends out his rays, so the Self sends out the Senses, and through them comes into contact with objects;

these objects are apprehended by the Mind, and are distinguished by their attributes as reached by the Senses; mental images consist of attributes, for the Mind cannot know objects except by their attributes. The Understanding concerns itself with these groups of attributes, or mental objects, and when it can get rid of the attributes and reach that in which they inhere, it attains to knowledge, and can then reflect the Self, which has knowledge as its essence. Mere intelligence, or Mind, at its highest, cannot behold the Self, nor can the Self be learned by teaching, since it cannot form the subject of language. It is reached by a reversal of the process by which it contacted the external world. The Senses are withdrawn from objects, and are placed, quiescent, in the Mind; the Mind is withdrawn from the images obtained by the aid of the Senses, and is placed, quiescent, in the Understanding. The Understanding withdraws itself from the study of attributes presented by the mind, and reflects the Self. This process of withdrawal is called yoga. The Senses cannot aid the Mind to become quiet, nor can the Mind apprehend the Understanding, nor the Understanding the manifested Self; the Self can know them all. The Mind should control the Senses; the Understanding should purify the mind; knowledge should cleanse the Understanding, and then the Self is reached. The mind may turn outwards to objects through the Senses, or inwards to the Self through the Understanding; the first course leads to misery, the second to bliss. [§ 202-206.] The Self is the Witness (§ 203), and is, in itself, inactive [§ 206]; but vivifying the ear, it hears; vivifying the eye, it sees; through the body it evolves its own nature, which is knowledge; and thus "the bodily organs are not the doers, but it is the Self that is the doer of all acts." [§ 210.] But as wind is not stained by the dust it carries away, but is separate from it, so is the Self unstained by actions, and separate from manifested life, existing in its own nature. Time is the cause of all we know as effects, of all multiplicity. [§ 211.]

Vrihaspati, speaking to Yudhishṭhira, laid down the fundamentals of true religion. "That man," said he, "who practises the religion of universal compassion, achieves his highest good......That man who regards all creatures as his own self, and behaves towards them as towards his own self, laying aside the rod of chastisement and completely subjugating his wrath, succeeds in attaining to happiness.....One should never do that to another which one regards as injurious to one's own self. This, in brief, is the rule of righteousness." [Anushâsana Parva, § 113.] This led king Yudhishṭhira to raise a question which is often heard now-a-days; should meat be eaten? Bhîshma answered that many discussions had taken place among the Ṛishis on this point, and their opinion was that abstention from meat was highly meritorious. "The self-born Manu has said, that that man who does not eat meat, or who does not slay living creatures, or who does not cause them to be slain, is a friend of all creatures. Such a man is incapable of being oppressed by any creature. He enjoys the confidence of all living beings. He always enjoys, besides, the approbation and commendation of the righteous. The righteous-souled Nârada has said that that man who wishes to increase his own flesh by eating the flesh of other creatures, meets with calamity.........That man who, having eaten meat, gives it up afterwards, acquires so great merit by such an act, that a study of all the Vedas, or a performance, O Bhârata, of all the sacrifices, cannot bestow its like. It is exceedingly difficult to give up meat, after one has become acquainted with its taste. Indeed, it is exceedingly difficult for such a person to observe the high vow of abstention from meat, a vow that assures every creature by dispelling all fear. That learned person, who giveth to all living creatures the dakshinâ [sacrificial gift] of complete assurance, doubtlessly comes to be regarded as the giver of life-breaths in this world. Even this is the high religion which men of wisdom praise. The life-breaths of other creatures are as dear to them as are one's own to oneself. Men endued with intelligence and of cleansed souls should always behave towards other creatures after the manner of that behaviour which they wish others to observe towards themselves....... Know that the discarding of meat is the highest refuge of religion, of heaven, and of happiness. Abstention from injury is the highest religion. It is again the highest penance. It is also the highest truth, from which all duty proceeds. Flesh cannot be had from grass or wood, or stone. Unless a living creature is slain, it cannot be had. Hence the fault of eating flesh." The killer, the purchaser, the eater are all sinful. Those who eat meat obtained from sacrifices, *i. e.* not slain for the gratification of taste, incur only a little fault. All other meat is gained by useless slaughter, and is therefore inedible by the good. "In this world there is nothing dearer to a creature than its life. Hence one should show compassion to the lives of others as one does to one's own life." Kshattriyas might eat meat obtained by hunting in which they risked their own lives: "there is equality of risk between the slayer and the slain." Moreover "the slayer is always slain." Karma returns to him his own acts. "Abstention from cruelty is the highest religion. Abstention from cruelty is the highest self-control. Abstention from cruelty is the highest gift," the highest penance, the highest sacrifice, the highest power, the highest friend, the highest happiness, the highest truth, the highest Scripture. "Gifts made in all sacrifices, ablutions performed in all sacred waters, and the merit acquired by making all the kinds of gifts mentioned in the Scriptures—all these do not come up to abstention from cruelty. The penances of a man that abstains from cruelty are inexhaustible. The man who abstains from cruelty is regarded as always performing sacrifices. The man who abstains from cruelty is the father and mother of all creatures." [§ 115, 116.]

Answering a question as to the God of the world, Bhîshma recited the thousand names of Vâsudeva [§ 149], and after some further discourse, he ceased, and the Great Exhortation was ended. As the vibrant voice sank into silence, a great stillness came down, and all the kings sat motionless, "like figures painted on canvas." Presently, at Vyâsa's suggestion, the great warrior bade Yudhishṭhira return home: "When the hour comes for my departure from this world, do thou come here, O king. The time when I shall take leave of my body is that period when the Sun, stopping in his southern course, will begin to return northwards." Reverently saluting Bhîshma, Yudhishṭhira returned to Hastinâpura, and remained there for fifty days, till the Sun turned to his northern path, and Bhîshma's departure was at hand. Then he collected all that was necessary for the burning of the body of the son of Gangâ, and the solemn procession set forth, bearing also with it his sacrificial fires. He found Bhîshma attended by Vyâsa and Nârada, Devala and Asita, with some monarchs that had remained, and, approaching the hero on his bed of arrows, he reverently told him that he had brought all that was needed for that appointed hour. Bhîshma opened his eyes, and greeted the young king lovingly, telling him that the hour had come, and then, turning to king Dhritarâshṭra, he bade him cherish the sons of Pâṇḍu and no longer grieve for his own children, and the Pâṇḍavas would dutifully serve and honour him. To Vâsudeva then the dying eyes turned in adoring love, and he hailed Him as the Holy One, the God of Gods; "Rescue me, O foremost of all beings. Do Thou give me permission, O Krishṇa, to depart from this world........ Do thou, O Krishṇa, grant me leave that I may cast off my body. Permitted by Thee, I shall attain to the highest end." The sweet music of Shrî

Krishṇa's voice fell melodiously on the expectant silence: "I give thee leave, O Bhîshma! Do thou, O king, attain to the region of the Vasus. O thou of great splendour, thou hast not been guilty of a single transgression in this world." Thus blessed by Keshava and declared blameless by Him who seeth all, Bhîshma bade farewell to his encircling friends his last words being for Yudhishṭhira. In silence for a while he lay, and then drew his life-breaths to the chakras one by one, till all were centred in the head. As he drew them upwards his body became as the body of a child, without wound or scar, and the radiant sheath of light, vivified by the life-breaths, pierced the crown of his head and rose triumphantly, ascending to the sky, while flowers rained down from heaven and celestial voices sang his praise. Thus "did Shântanu's son, that pillar of Bharata's race, unite himself with the Eternal." [§ 166-168.]

——:0:——

CHAPTER IX.

The Closing Scenes.

When king Yudhishṭhira was mounting the bank of Gangâ, after libations had been offered to Bhîshma, his grief overcame him and he fell, "like an elephant pierced by the hunter." Very tenderly Govinda consoled him, telling him that overmuch sorrow grieved those who had departed, and then Vyâsa bade him celebrate the Horse Sacrifice, the Ashvamedha, which gives the name to this Parva and give gifts, thus removing his grief and obtaining prosperity. Yudhishṭhira objecting that his treasury was empty and that he could not levy on his impoverished kingdom, Vyâsa told him that he could find vast stores of gold in the Himâlayas, left there after the sacrifice offered by a king, whose story he related. To calm Yudhishṭhira, Vâsudeva explained to him that he must conquer sorrow by mastering his mind: "The time has now arrived when thou must fight the battle which each must fight single-handed with his mind... In this war there will be no need for any missiles, nor for friends nor attendants. The battle which is to be fought alone and single-handed has now arrived for thee. If vanquished in this struggle, thou shalt find thyself in the most wretched plight. O son of Kuntî, knowing this and acting accordingly, shalt thou attain success." Then Yudhishṭhira struggled against his despondency, and, gratefully thanking his consolers, betook himself to his duties, returning to Hastinâpura. [§ 1-14.]

Shrî Krishṇa and Arjuna now for awhile travelled together in pleasant places in peace and joy [§ 15], and one day Arjuna reminded his divine Friend of the teaching He had given him just before the battle. This he had forgotten, and he prayed the Lord to again instruct him. Vâsudeva replied gravely and reproachfully that He had then told him mysterious and eternal truths, having concentrated Himself in Yoga, and that He could not now remember all that He had then said. He would, however, recite to him an ancient history of what a Brâhmaṇa, visiting heaven, had said concerning emancipation. This discourse is the famous "Anugîtâ" [§ 16-51], in which, as Vâsudeva told Arjuna, "I am the preceptor, O mighty armed one, and know that the mind is My pupil." This is another of the profound teachings which you must one day study.

Then Shrî Kṛishṇa, desiring to return home, drove to Hastinâpura with Arjuna, and having obtained

Yudhishṭhira's permission to leave, He bade farewell to the Pâṇḍavas and Kurus, and, taking His sister Subhadrâ with him, departed to Dvârakâ. There He was welcomed with great joy, and recounted the story of the great battle to Vasudeva and Devakî; a pathetic scene occurred when He told the tale of Abhimanyu's death, omitted by Him at first in compassionate tenderness, and described the courage with which Kuntî had borne the terrible blow, and had cheered her widowed grand-daughter. [§ 52-61.]

Meanwhile, in Hastinâpura, Yudhishṭhira, urged by Vyâsa, was preparing for the Horse Sacrifice, and presently set out with his brothers and a large train to the Himâlayas; having worshipped Mahâdeva, he made excavations on the spot where the wealth had been buried, and dug out vast stores of coins and vessels, which he brought back by slow marches to his capital. [§ 62-65.] During his absence, Keshava returned to Hastinâpura, for the time had come for the birth of Abhimanyu's son, and soon the child was born, but born dead, slain by the celestial weapon of Ashvatthâmâ. Hastily Shrî Krishṇa entered the inner apartments, to be met by Kuntî and Subhadrâ and many others, weeping piteously, and crying to Him for help. His sister, wailing, reminded Him of His promise to revive the child, and prayed Him to fulfil it: "If only Thou wishest it, Thou canst revive the three worlds, if dead. What need I say, therefore, of this darling child, born but dead, of Thy sister's son." Clearly came the assenting answer, "So be it!" and the Lord passed on into the room where the newly made mother sat, with her dead son in her arms, and was greeted by Uttarâ with piteous reverence and appeal. Pathetically she called on her babe to rise and greet the Lord of the worlds, and then, controlling herself with strong patience, she waited Govinda's mercy. And He, the merciful and mighty, spake His word of power: "O Uttarâ! I never utter an untruth. My words will prove true. I shall revive this child in the presence of all creatures. Never have I uttered an untruth, even in jest. Never have I turned back from battle. Let this child revive! As righteousness is dear to me, as Brâhmaṇas are especially dear to me, let Abhimanyu's son, who is born dead, revive! Never hath a misunderstanding arisen between Me and My friend Vijaya [Arjuna]. Let this dead child revive by that troth. As truth and righteousness are always established in Me, let this dead child of Abhimanyu revive. As Kansa and Keshi have been righteously slain by Me, let this child revive to-day by that truth." As the sweet voice ceased, the dead child revived and began to move, and cries of praise and joy took the place of sobs and wailings. And Keshava named the child, when the right time came, saying: "Since this child of Abhimanyu has been born at a time when this race hath become nearly extinct, let his name be Parikshit" (all round decayed). A month later the Pâṇḍavas arrived, bringing home the wealth they had collected. [§ 66-70.]

Preparations for the great sacrifice were now rapidly made, and Arjuna was chosen to follow and guard the sacrificial steed. A magnificent black horse was chosen, and, Yudhishṭhira having been duly initiated as the performer of the sacrifice, the steed was set loose to wander whither he would. Every king whose land he entered must either acknowledge Yudhishṭhira as lord, or do battle with the black steed's champion, and none might check or stay him save at his peril. Arjuna followed in his war-chariot, to which were yoked white horses, as was his wont, and the twain, steed and champion, set forth amid the plaudits and blessings of all. In the course of his wanderings and fightings, Arjuna came to the dominions of Manipura, the ruler of which was his own son; the king came to meet his father with submissive reverence, but Arjuna told him sternly that he was behaving like a woman instead of like a Kshattriya and must fight him for his crown. Ulûpî, the daughter of the Snake King, appeared, and incited the young king, Babhruvâhana, to do battle with his father, and a fierce duel began, in which the youth showed great courage and skill, to the delight of Arjuna; finally Arjuna fell, under a well-aimed shaft, and his son swooned on seeing his father's fall. Then Chitrângadâ, his mother, came hastily to the field, and reproached Ulûpî for having encouraged the combat, declaring that she would starve herself to death if Ulûpî did not revive their husband, Arjuna. Babhruvâhana, recovering from his swoon, added his prayers to those of his mother, and took a similar vow of death by starvation, till Ulûpî, thinking of a gem that could revive the dead, called that gem to her by her thought. Then she told the young king that he could not really conquer Arjuna, but that she had caused an illusion for Arjuna's sake, and that if he placed the jewel on Arjuna's breast he would revive. When the hero arose, he asked wonderingly what had happened, and Ulûpî told him that the Vasus had cursed him because he had shot Bhîshma unrighteously when he was not battling with him; Ulûpî, deeply grieved, had sought her father's help, who went to the Vasus and pacified them, so that they agreed that Arjuna should fall before his own son, and thus be freed from their curse, expiating his fault. Then Arjuna bade his son come to the sacrifice, and went on his way through the lands, until at last he saw again the walls of Hastinâpura, and was welcomed home again in triumph, his task achieved. [§ 71-81.]

Vast was the wealth expended in that sacrifice, the arches, ornamental stakes, jars and vessels being all of gold, and myriads of golden coins being given away. To Vyâsa, the king gave the conquered earth as gift, declaring his wish to go away into the woods. But Vyâsa bade him redeem the earth with gold, and he yielded to the command, and all who attended the sacrifice, from Brâhmaṇas to Mlechchas, returned home laden with wealth. But a curious thing happened. A mongoose, half of whose body was golden, appeared and said: "Ye kings, this great sacrifice is not equal to a little measure of powdered barley given away by a liberal Brâhmaṇa of Kurukshetra, who was observing the unccha vow." Questioned as to the meaning of his strange words, the mongoose told the following story: There was a Brâhmaṇa who, with his family, was living on the grains of corn he could pick up in the fields, eating but once a day at a fixed hour. And behold! a terrible famine laid waste the land, and it chanced many times that at the meal time no food was to be had, and the man, his wife, his son and his daughter-in-law grew thin and weak, till they were mere living skeletons. Now one day the Brâhmaṇa picked up some barley, and, powdering it, they were about to sit down to eat it, having divided it into four portions. At that moment came a guest, and, welcoming him, they gave him water and a seat, and then the Brâhmaṇa gave him his share of food. The guest ate it, but was still hungry, and the wife brought her share to her husband and prayed him to feed with it their guest. Seeing her shaking with the weakness of starvation, he gently bade her keep it, but she pleaded sweetly till he gave it, and still the guest's hunger was unappeased. Then the son brought his share, dutifully urging his claim to share his father's hunger, and the Brâhmaṇa gave it smilingly to his hungry guest. Alas! he was still hungry, having eaten it, and what remained? Only the young wife's share, and that it broke her father's heart to give, the food of the tender child he loved so well. Yet her sacrifice was made with such grace of sweet humility that, blessing her, he took it and gave it to his guest, and lo! that guest arose in dazzling radiance of divinity, and it was Dharma whom they had fed. And the God praised and blessed them, in that they had kept righteousness unstained, and bade them rise in happy peace to heaven. And the mongoose, coming where some grains of the barley-powder had fallen, rolled on them and half his body turned to gold from the magic power of that loving sacrifice, and ever after had he sought a sacrifice of equal merit and had found none, no, not that sacrifice of king Yudhishṭhira, with all its gorgeous profusion of gold and gems. [§ 88-92.]

The Âshramavâsika Parva gives the closing scenes of the life of Dhritarâshṭra, Gândhârî and Kuntî. For fifteen years the blind king dwelt in peace and honour, obeyed by Yudhishṭhira and his brothers, who surrounded him with the tenderest reverence, that, deprived of all his children, he might never feel neglected or unhappy. Alone Bhîma still cherished hatred in his heart, and, though outwardly reverent in his behaviour, he would secretly try to make trouble, and would utter bitter speeches within the hearing of the blind king, who was often thus pierced to the heart. At last Dhritarâshṭra called his nephews, and confessed to them his secret penances for the faults that had brought about the war, praying Yudhishṭhira to consent to his retiring with his wife to the forest, to close his life in asceticism. Yudhisṭhira answered lovingly, praying him to remain, but the old king, repeating his wish, fainted away from weakness, induced by age and much fasting. Great was Yudhishṭhira's sorrow, but Vyâsa came and bade him yield to his uncle's request, reminding him that death in battle or in the forest was the fitting close for a royal Kshattriya's life. So Yudhishṭhira yielded, though sad at heart, and the brothers assembled, to hear the last instructions of the old king ere he left them. Having exhorted Yudhishṭhira on the discharge of his royal duties, Dhritarâshṭra rested for awhile, and then addressed the citizens, summoned at his wish. He spoke affectionately to them, telling them that being old and childless, he wished to retire to the woods with his wife; he had striven to serve them, but, through his son's fault and his own, great carnage had occurred, for which he prayed their forgiveness. Yudhishṭhira would rule them well, and he gave him the realm in charge. Let them forgive and forget any injury done them by his dead sons, and give him permission to retire. The crowd listened to the pathetic pleading of the aged and grief-stricken monarch with streaming eyes, unable to speak in answer, and Dhritarâshṭra again uttered a few broken words, begging for his release from royal duties. At last a Brâhmaṇa was put forward to speak, who voiced the love and gratitude of the people, and declared that Dhritarâshṭra and his sons were honoured by them as true monarchs of men; let the king go forth in peace, and accomplish his righteous wish. [§ 1-10.]

Dhritarâshṭra then decided to leave on the approaching full moon of Kârtika, and, ere going, asked the Pânḍavas to give him wealth that he might perform the Shrâddha of Bhîshma and other heroes. Yudhishṭhira and Arjuna gladly consented, declaring that they and all they possessed were his; alone Bhîma grudged the giving, despite the gentle pleading of Arjuna and the rebuke of his elder brother. He could not blot out from his memory the bitter wrongs and sufferings of the past. At last all was over, the last splendid gifts were made, royally closing a royal life, and then Dhritarâshṭra set forth on foot, trembling with weakness and leaning on his devoted wife, from the city he had ruled so long Vidura and Sanjaya accompanied him, as did also Kuntî, despite the passionate lamentations and protests of her sons, and the sad procession moved through crowds of grief-stricken people, till the city was left behind, and the blind king and his followers passed out of sight. But the Pânḍavas could not be comforted for the loss of their mother, and grieved for her incessantly. At length they resolved to visit their loved ones in their forest retreat, and, going forth, found them and fell at their feet, embracing them, and abode with them for a brief space. Vidura not being present, Yudhishṭhira enquired for him, and as Dhritarashṭra was answering, Vidura was seen at a distance. Yudhishṭhira sprang up to meet him, but Vidura turned and fled, pursued by the young king, crying to him, till they reached a lonely spot, where Vidura stopped and leaned against a tree. Yudhishṭhira bowed down before him, and Vidura gazed steadily at him, and, so continuing to gaze, passed into a yoga-trance, and, entering the body of Yudhishṭhira, he united his life with that of the young king, who felt his own life enriched, and then remembered his own state before his present birth. Thus Vidura passed away from his body, obtaining a lofty heavenly life, and Yudhishṭhira returned back and related all that had occurred. [§ 11-26.]

The Pâṇḍavas had spent about a month with the ascetics when Vyâsa came thither; on his questioning Dhritarâshṭra as to the grief that still burned within him, Dhritarâshṭra confessed that he was ever anxious as to the fate of his sons, who had brought about the slaughter of Bhîshma and Droṇa and of so many others. Kuntî also confessed her longing to see Karṇa, her eldest son, and Gândhârî breathed her deep yearning to know the fate of her children, speaking also for Krishṇâ, Subhadrâ, and the other bereaved wives and mothers. Then Vyâsa told them that the great warriors who had fallen in battle were all Rishis, Gandharvas, Râkshasas, and other Suras and Asuras, who had taken birth for this struggle, and on the coming night, on the banks of Gangâ, they should see their dead again. And that night, Vyâsa, standing in the stream, called on the warriors who had passed though death to appear, and they came in all the glory of their heavenly state, radiant, full of peace and joy. Then Karṇa was reconciled with the Pâṇḍavas, and Abhimanyu and the children of Draupadî gladdened their mothers' hearts, and the warriors all met in amity, all past strifes forgotten. Great was the rejoicing, measureless the content, in that night's blest reunion, and, on the leaving of the heroes, their wives, casting off their bodies, accompanied them to the regions of happiness. Shortly after this, the Pâṇḍavas bade farewell to Dhritarâshṭra, Gândhârî and Kuntî—despite a last attempt of Yudhishṭhira and Sahadeva to remain with them—and departed to Hastinâpura, whither came Nârada, two years later, to announce the passing of the three royal ascetics. He told them that, after practising severe austerities, they had gone to the banks of Gangâ, Sanjaya accompanying them. As they turned away, they beheld the forest in flames before them, and Dhritarâshṭra, bidding Sanjaya leave them, sat down with Gândhârî and Kuntî, to await the end. There, absorbed in meditation, they were burned in a conflagration kindled by their own sacrificial fires, abandoned in the woods, and they thus passed to the heavenly worlds. And though Yudhishṭhira, thinking of his mother, wept like a child, raising his arms in agony, yet he, with his brothers, regained calmness, soothed by Nârada, and, though sad, bore patiently the heavy burden of sovereignty. Now eighteen years had passed since the great battle, when Dhritarâshṭra cast off his body. [§ 27-39.]

The Mausala Parva, in its eight sections, tells of the slaughter of the race of Keshava, and of the departure from earth of Balarâma and Shrî Krishṇa. Thirtysix years had come and gone since the struggle on the field of Kuru, and strange portents appeared on every side, the lord of day grew dim, and blazing circles were seen round sun and moon. Moved by folly, the hour of doom having struck, some heroes of the Vrishnis, seeing the approach of Nârada, Vishvâmitra and Kanna, dressed up Shâmva, a warrior, as a woman, and asked the sages what this woman, desiring a son, should bring forth. "A fierce iron bolt," was the stern answer, "for the destruction of the Vrishnis and Andhakas." On the following day, an iron bolt came forth from Shâmva's body, and the king Upasarga, to avoid the foretold fate, ground it into powder and cast it into the sea. But lo! many dread omens appeared, foreboding the coming doom. The discus of Shrî Krishṇa ascended to heaven, and His famous horses fled away with His celestial car under the very eyes of His charioteer, while His standard and that of Balarâma were carried away by Apsaras. And patiently He waited, knowing all that was to come. Then one day the Vrishni heroes gave themselves up to drinking, and, excited by wine, they flung taunts at each other, Sâtyaki jeering at Kritavarman for the midnight raid on the camp of the sleeping hosts of the sons of Pâṇḍu. Bitter speeches were exchanged, while Govinda sat silently waiting, till Sâtyaki rushed at Kritavarman and severed his head from his body, and a fierce fight ensued. Keshava, presently stooping, took up a handful of grass, and it changed into a terrible bolt of iron, and He stood there with the bolt uplifted, eyeing in sad stern silence all that passed, while blades of grass in the hands of the combatants became bolts of iron, until His bolt flew forth and all was done, and he stood, with two survivors, amid the dead. Then Govinda sent one of these,

His charioteer, Dâruka, to tell Arjuna to come thither, and was sending the second to see to the women of the household, when he was struck dead: so, placing these under his father's care, He went forth alone and joined His elder brother Râma in the forest. And behold! Râma sat, immersed in yoga, and out of his mouth was issuing a mighty snake, and that was Shesha, the eternal Serpent, who had dwelt as Râma in the world, and now went forth, returning to his own place. Then Shrî Krishṇa wandered on alone, knowing that His hour was come, and, willing to die as men die, He laid Himself down on the ground, leaving His feet exposed—for only the soles of His feet were vulnerable. Wrapped in His yellow robes He lay, fixed in yoga, and a passing hunter, deeming he saw a couchant deer, pierced His heel with a shaft. Then approaching, he saw that he had pierced the Lord, and fell at His feet afraid, but Keshava spoke words of comfort to him, and then rose upward, filling the heaven with His splendour; and hosts of celestial beings came flocking to give Him welcome, hymning the Lord, returning to His own heavenly region, and He rose onwards, gladdening the heavens with His glory, but leaving desolate the bereaved and lonely earth.

And Arjuna, His well-beloved, what of Arjuna? Receiving Keshava's message, he set out at once for Dvârakâ, and found the fair city in lamentation, widowed of joy, and Keshava departed, none knew whither. All that Vasudeva could say was that his divine Son had left him, telling that Arjuna would come and do all that was needed for the women and children, and that on his departure Dvârakâ would be swallowed up by the sea. On the morrow's dawning, the aged Vasudeva passed away. and was burned with great honour by Arjuna, who seeking for the cast-off bodies of Râma and Keshava, caused them also to be burned. On the seventh day he left Dvârakâ, escorting the mournful procession of widows and orphans. As they left, the ocean rose and overwhelmed Shrî Krishṇa's much loved home, and the mourners pressed on more rapidly in front of the swelling waves. As they travelled, they were one day assailed by robbers, and Arjuna, laughiug at their insolence, turned to drive them away. Alas! what is this? Gâṇḍîva will scarce bend to her mighty master's hand, and for the first time resists his stringing. His celestial weapons come not at his calling, his shafts, erewhile inexhaustible, are exhausted. Under the very eyes of the conqueror of Kurukshetra, many a sweet woman is dragged into captivity, and robbers overcome him before whom warrior-kings had fled. Ashamed, he yielded and went on his way, taking the remnant of the women and the wealth, and settling them in various cities of his brother's realm. Then he sought Vyâsa and at his feet poured out his sorrows: the Vrishnis were slain; his weapons had failed him; Râma and Keshava had cast off Their bodies. His Govinda's death was as incredible as the drying up of the ocean, or the falling down of heaven; reft of Govinda, how could he live? Keshava had left the the earth, and his heart was empty. Gravely and steadily Vyâsa spoke: The great work of the Gods was performed; what need for grief? He and his brothers had done their work, and the time had come for their departure. The weapons had gone back to their own place, being no longer needed. The time for liberation was here. Then Arjuna departed to Hastinâpura, and recounted all that had happened. [§ 1-8.]

The shadows deepen round the heroic brothers, and the Great Going Forth is here. In three brief sections the Mahâprasthânika Parva tells the pathetic tale. Yudhishṭhira, hearing Arjuna's story, declared that the time had come for them to go, and Arjuna sadly sighed, "Time, time!" like the tolling of a funeral knell. The three other brothers agreeing, Parikshit was made king of the Kurus in Hastinâpura, and the sole surviving Yâdava prince, Vajra, was installed as ruler of Indraprastha. Kripa was was made Guru of Parikshiṭ, and Yuyutsu, the only remaining royal warrior of the elder generation, was placed in charge of the kingdom. This done, the five brothers and their wife clad themselves in robes of bark, and set forth from Hastinâpura for the last time, recalling the similar leaving after the game of dice, but now, though the onlookers were weeping, the brothers were smiling, for they were glad at heart in casting off the burden of royalty, no longer prized. And a seventh followed them—a dog. One behind the other they walked, Yudhishṭhira first and the others in the order of their birth, while Draupadî followed Sahadeva, and the dog came last of all. Arjuna still carried Gâṇḍîva and his quivers, loth to part with them, but when, after long travel eastwards, they reached the sea, Agni, the seven-flamed, stood before them, and bade Arjuna cast his weapons in the sea, that Varuṇa might take them back in charge. Then Arjuna cast them in ; his last bond with earth was broken.

Far they journeyed southward, and then southwest and west, and then turned their weary feet northward to where Himâlaya lifts his awful peaks to heaven. Crossing the mighty range, they saw stretching in front of them a vast sandy desert, and beyond was Meru, the ancient, the monarch of mountains. Silently they walked across the sandy waste, till suddenly Draupadî fell, to rise no more. Then on the silence rose the grieved voice of Bhîma, asking his elder brother why Krishṇâ had fallen. "She was partial in her love, placing first Dhananjaya. She obtains the fruit of that partiality to-day." And steadily Yudhisṭhira walked onward, while Krishṇâ lay alone. Then Sahadeva fell, and rose not, and Bhîma questioned of his fate. "He never thought any one his equal in wisdom. For that fault falls the prince." And Yudhishṭhira stayed not, but walked steadfastly on. Presently the loving heart of Nakula broke for dead Krishṇâ and his twin-brother, and he fell silently. Bhîma cried to his brother that Nakula had fallen; "He thought that none equalled him in beauty," answered the firm-souled king, and stepped forward undismayed. But see! now Arjuna falls, the hero, the invincible; Ah, why? mourns Bhîma. "Arjuna said he would consume all our foes in a single day. Proud was he in his heroism, but he did not what he boasted. Hence has he fallen down." And still with steady heart the king goes on. Then Bhîma falls, and his voice rings out again. "O king, behold! I, who am thy darling, have dropped down. For what reason have I fallen? Tell me, if thou knowest." Without looking back, Yudhishṭhira answers: "Thou wert a great eater, and thou didst oft boast of thy strength. Thou didst never, O Pârtha! attend to the wants of others while eating. For that, O Bhîma, hast thou fallen down." Unshaken, though now alone, the king, walks on. Alone? nay, still his dog follows him, faithful to the end.

But list! a rattle as of thunder, and down flashes Indra on a celestial chariot, and bids the king ascend in it to heaven. Nay, that he will not do. His brothers, fallen by the way, and his sweet Krishṇâ; not without them will he ascend to heaven. Then Indra tells him they are gone thither before him, but in his body must he rise to Svarga. What now prevents? why does he hesitate? "This dog, O Lord of the past and present, is very devoted to me. He should go with me. My heart is full of compassion for him." But Indra will have none of the dog: "Immortality and a condition equal to mine, O king, far-stretching prosperity, and high success, and all the joys of heaven—these hast thou won to-day. Cast off this dog. There is nothing cruel in the act." Steadily sounds the voice of the white-souled king: "O thou of a thousand eyes, O thou of righteous behaviour, an Aryan cannot do an act unworthy of an Aryan.

I do not desire a bliss bought by casting off one who is devoted to me." "There is no place in heaven for persons with dogs," says Indra; "abandon the dog!" "It is said the abandonment of one that is devoted is infinitely sinful. It is equal to the sin incurred by slaying a Brâhmaṇa. O great Indra, not for the sake of my own happiness shall I cast away this dog!" Still Indra urges him; he had renounced his brothers and Krishṇâ, why not a dog? O righteous king! unshaken in the hour of temptation; now comes out the value of the lesson learned on Kurukshetra in his fall from truth. Not for the joys of heaven, not for the urging of a God, will he swerve from righteousness: "This is well known in all the worlds that there is neither friendship nor enmity with the dead. When my brothers and Krishṇâ died, I was unable to revive them. Hence it was that I abandoned them. I did not abandon them as long as they were living. To terrorise one who has sought protection, to slay a woman, to steal what is a Brâhmaṇa's, to injure a friend, each of these, methinks, is equal, O Shakra, to the abandonment of one who is devoted." Then the dog vanishes, and, radiantly glorious, Dharma arises from his form, and blesses his son for this bright example of compassion and faithfulness; believing the dog to be faithfu he had renounced the very chariot of the Gods rather than abandon him; "Regions of inexhaustible joy are thine. Thou hast won them, O king, and thine is a high and a celestial goal." Then Yudhishṭhira, with Indra and Dharma and many other Gods, ascends in triumph to heaven, while Nârada proclaims him greatest of royal sages. But in the midst of this intoxicating glory, Yudhishṭhira's loving faithful heart yearns for his brothers and his wife. "Happy or woeful," he cries, "I desire to go to the region that is now my brothers'; I do not wish to go anywhere else." Vainly Indra bids him leave all human affections, and enjoy the heavenly kingdom he has won; his brothers are happy; let them be. But no! where is Draupadî? there must he also be; "O conqueror of Daityas, I venture not to dwell anywhere, separated from them. I desire to go whither my brothers have gone." [§ 1-3.]

Unsatisfied, the longing eyes of Yudhishṭhira turned from face to face in heaven. Nowhere he saw the loved features his heart desired. Then his gaze fell on one he sought not: lo! Duryodhana was there! Indignantly he cried out in protest; he did not wish even to see his old foe, and again his yearning broke forth: "I wish to go there where my brothers are!" Nârada told him, smiling, that there were no enmities in heaven, but Yudhishṭhira would not be turned from his search for his brothers, for Karṇa, for the heroes who had died in his quarrel: "I wish not to stay here. I tell you the truth. Ye foremost ones among the Gods, what is heaven to me if I am separated from my brothers? That is heaven where my brothers are. This is not heaven for me." Then the Gods bade a heavenly messenger lead Yudhishṭhira to his brothers and his friends, and they turned their backs on heaven and set forth. Darker and darker grew the path, gloomier the shadows gathered round. Foul things of noisome smell and evil shape crowded around them as they went, the ground was slippery with blood and strewn with fragments of the corpses of men. Sharp thorns and piercing leaves obstructed it, and burning sand, and iron stones white-hot. Astounded, the king questioned his celestial guide, who told him that thus far he had been bidden lead him, and if he were weary, he might return. Slowly Yudhishṭhira turned back, but as he turned, piteous lamentations broke out around him, and voices prayed him to stay awhile, as his sweet presence eased the torments; even for a few moments let him stay. Then the merciful-souled king paused in compassion, and, standing still, cried out: "Who are you?" What are the moans that answer to his words? "I am Karṇa." "I am Bhîshma."

"I am Arjuna." "I am Nakula." "I am Sahadeva.' "I am Dhrishṭadyumna." "I am Draupadî." "We are the sons of Draupadî." Ye just Gods! what is this? Duryodhana in heaven, and these heroes here! Bewilderment, grief, at last anger, sweep over the king's heart. "Return," he cries to the heavenly messenger, "return to the presence of those whose messenger thou art. Tell them I shall not return to them, but shall stay here, even here, since by my presence these tortured brothers of mine are comforted." O noble heart! O spotless loyalty and dauntless courage! And lo! in a moment the Gods are there, with Indra at their head, and all the horrors vanish like an evil dream, and all is light and fragrance and balmy airs. Then Indra speaks and comforts the saddened king, telling him that these illusions are over, and that he and his brothers had but seen hell by illusion; his sin against Droṇa brought on him this brief deception, this passing misery. Now let him rise to heaven where all his brothers are awaiting him, and reap in joy the fruits of all his woe. And Dharma speaks, praising his noble son, and bids him plunge into the heavenly Gangâ, wherein bathing, he casts off his human body and assumes a heavenly form.

Then comes the joy of re-union, for there is

Govinda in blazing glory, He who the Friend on earth, and with Him Arjuna, His beloved, radiant and adoring Him. And in another place with Sûrya Karṇa is shining, refulgent in golden glory, and Bhîma elsewhere rejoices with Vâyu, and the Ashvins have with them Nakula and Sahadeva, while Krishṇâ is again the Goddess Shrî, and Abhimanyu is shining with the silver radiance of night's bright God. Pânḍu is there, with Kuntî and Mâdrî, and Bhîshma is restored to his place among the Vasus, while Droṇa lives beside Vrihaspati. Sorrow is exhausted, and all, at last, is joy. [Svargârohaṇika Parva, § 1-5.]

Thus the story of the Great War hath ending, and all strifes are merged in peace.

PEACE TO ALL BEINGS.

——:o:——

Treasure of Books

Under One Roof

Demand

Any Rare Book

at

www.facsimilepublishers.com

Demand Any Rare Book at:

www.facsimilepublishers.com

if not available, give information,
our team will search and update you.

Promote Knowledge:

If you have any rare book
which is not available at
www.facsimilepublishers.com,
offer it to other readers so that others can also be
benefitted with your cooperation.
The book will be printed with your courtesy.

Print & Publish:

If you wish to get your book printed or published,
we have the service for you.

Customization on Demand:

We offer customization of books
as per the demand of the customer.

Published by

Facsimile Publisher
Ashok Vihar, Delhi-110052 (India)
Website: www.facsimilepublishers.com

Distributed by

Gyan Books Pvt. Ltd.
5, Ansari Road, Daryaganj, New Delhi-110002 (India)
E-mail: books@gyanbooks.com, Website: www.gyanbooks.com

9 789333 037129